DESIGN

A CRASH
COURSE

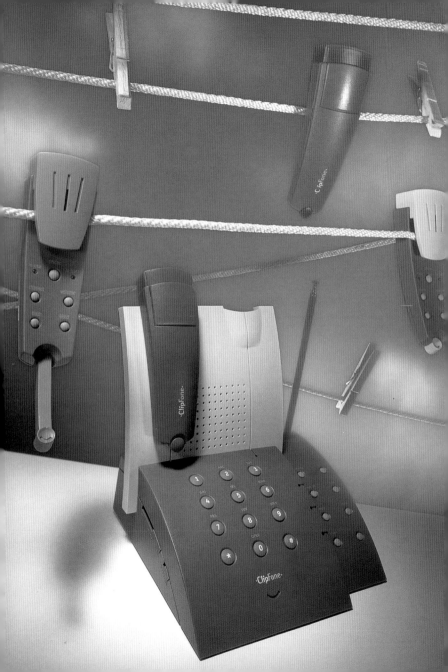

DESIGN

A CRASH
COURSE

PAUL CLARK
JULIAN FREEMAN

WATSON-GUPTILL
PUBLICATIONS
New York

First published in the United States in 2000
by Watson-Guptill Publications, a division of
BPI Communications, Inc., 1515 Broadway,
New York, NY 10036

Library of Congress
Catalog Card Number: 99-09642

ISBN 0-8230-0983-1

*This book was conceived, designed,
and produced by*
THE IVY PRESS LIMITED
The Old Candlemakers, West Street
Lewes, East Sussex, BN7 2NZ, England

Art Director: PETER BRIDGEWATER
Editorial Director: DENNY HEMMING
Designer: JANE LANAWAY
Editor: PETER NICKOL
DTP Designers: CHRIS LANAWAY, TRUDI VALTER
Illustrations: IVAN HISSEY
Picture Researcher: VANESSA FLETCHER

Printed and bound in China by
Hong Kong Graphic and Printing Ltd.

1 2 3 4 5 6 7 8 9 / 08 07 06 05 04 03 02 01 00
This book is typeset in Bauer Bodoni 8/11.

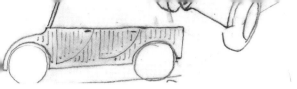

Contents

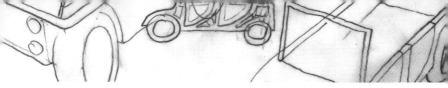

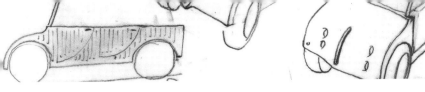

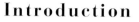

Introduction

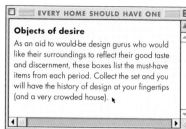

Essentially this book is about Things, and the history of Things. We human beings have become very good at making things—just look around you—and every single one of those things has an element of Design involved in its making.

We needn't get too hung up about the exact meaning of that word "design." It may encompass invention, or artistry. It may also encompass an initial idea. Design tends to overlap with all these elements at one time or another, and any boundaries we draw will be somewhat artificial. Did the German Konrad Gesner design the pencil in 1565, or invent it? Did the 19-year-old French mathematical genius Blaise Pascal invent, or design, the first efficient calculating machine in 1642? Was Toulouse-Lautrec an artist, or (sometimes) a poster designer?

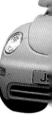

Nineteenth-century poster design by the little maestro Toulouse-Lautrec.

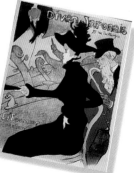

Even the pencil had to start on someone's drawing board.

"Design" can mean or imply many different things. It is certainly concerned with how things look, but also with how things work. If the emphasis is on the former, we might think of that as "decorative design"; if on the latter, we call it "functional design."

How this course works
Begin at the beginning, carry on to the end, and then stop. Of course, design is a continuous and continuing process, but this chronology of Thing-making covers all the important figures and events, with regular features to fill in the gaps.

Almost every design involves some balance of appearance and function, from the vases of ancient Greece to the latest status-symbol car. In terms of materials and scale, the need for design crosses the whole range of human endeavor: everything from microchips to giant engineering and architectural plans. So it's a huge field, and a "designer" might be doing any one of many different jobs.

The Beetle in its latest incarnation, a simple design that has stood the test of time.

An important watershed in the history of design occurred at the time of the Industrial Revolution, in the late

Greek ceramic kylix featuring a plowing scene, c. 550 BC.

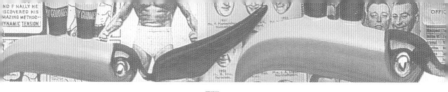

Topiary, a specialized branch (sorry) of garden design.

eighteenth century. Before it, when things were hand-made, they continually varied; sometimes the variations were deliberate, but more often they were accidental. As soon as things were made by machines, their design needed to be more consciously planned and fixed. It is no accident that technical drawing was first used in the 1790s.

Recent decades have seen the word "design" being adopted by all kinds of people: hairdressers have become "hair designers"; interior decorators have become "interior designers"; and of course gardeners have become "garden designers." Design has become inextricably mixed up with street style, upward mobility, and extravagant consumption. Sometimes it seems to be assumed that "designed" or "designer" automatically means "well designed" or "good designer." Like the man said, it ain't necessarily so.

Nevertheless, design influences every aspect of our lives. Whether we are relaxing, traveling, or working, we are surrounded by designed things.

The human world is a designed world.

How did all these things come about? When, and why? What are they made of, and how well do they work? And who were the people responsible?

This is the story of design, the story of the making of Things.

P.B. Clark

The Picasso Internet audio concept, which lets you listen to Internet-based music wherever you are. Now that's progress…

An iMac rainbow—you can have one for each day of the working week.

PAUL CLARK

1.75 million B.C.
Chopper tools are used near Olduvai Gorge, Tanzania, for breaking up carcasses and scraping vegetation.

75,000 B.C.
Neanderthal humans can communicate using speech, setting them apart from other animals.

42,000 B.C. The continent that will be called Australia is populated by the earth's first seafaring people. Colonists arrive from the Asian mainland.

Year Dot~5000 B.C.

I Think, Therefore I Design
First made things

How would you have liked it? No clothes, no kitchen, no dishes, no refrigerator, no central heating. No fire, and an ice age coming on. Do you become a meal for a saber-toothed tiger, or do you solve your problems through design?

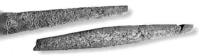

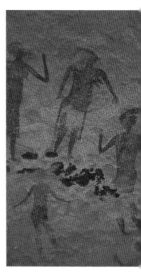

Paleolithic horn spearheads found at Willendorf, Austria.

Cave painting showing the dress taste of early men and women, from Jabbaren, Algeria.

Our ancestors had to design and make all the things they needed to help them survive. All they had to do it with was stones, skins, bones, sticks, leaves, and stems—and more stones (the reason that there are so many stone tools in museums is because they don't rot). By adapting the raw materials around them, the first humans started on the path that leads to our present-day accomplishments (and failings). The first inklings of design ideas helped them to provide food and shelter and the weapons that enabled them to compete with more powerful animal predators, and with the tribe over the hill. In the beginning, designing and making were virtually the same activity.

If you go along with the theory of evolution, the slight survival advantage that the first steps of tool making gave our forebears gradually encouraged the development of humankind along that route. We have subsequently distanced ourselves from "nature" in our efforts to improve our chances in the material world.

Can animals design things?
Animals certainly build things such as nests and webs, but they don't do it consciously. Instead, they work according to inbuilt instructions that have taken millions of years to evolve.

HELP YOURSELF TO A FLINT, THEY'RE FREE
The earliest known designed things that have survived are stone tools (from 2.5 million years ago): knives, scrapers, and axes. Many perishable materials—leaves, sticks, vines, and skin—would also have

25,000 B.C.
Fishermen in Europe's Dordogne Valley develop the first fishing lines, made from plant fibers.

13,600 B.C. A Great Flood covers much of the world following a 130-foot rise in sea levels due to the melting of a glacial ice sheet over the Western Hemisphere's northern continent.

6000 B.C. Humans develop the first real pottery, permitting new ways of cooking.

been used. Natural objects such as shells and gourds served as basic vessels and containers. Just think: the first person who rinsed a shell in a stream invented dish washing.

KEEPING UP APPEARANCES

While they embarked on the path that led to the mobile phone, our ancestors demonstrated another very human trait—an interest in the look of things, including themselves. The oldest known clothing is 33,000 years old—fur pants and a shirt found in Russia.

From about 25,000 years ago, at about the same time as remarkable cave paintings were being created, there seems to have been a burst of human creativity and a developing pride

The voluptuous "Venus of Willendorf," a sandstone statuette dating from about 20,000 B.C.

Name that age

For convenience we have named the prehistoric periods by the main material that was being exploited at the time. Each of these marked a new technology that people had mastered, giving the possibility of new, improved things. The European Stone Age started approximately 30,000 years ago, followed 10,000 years ago by the Bronze Age, and then 3,000 years ago by the Iron Age.

in craftsmanship. This is reflected in the earliest "status" burials of this period, which contain decorative possessions, such as necklaces, which were obviously seen as important to their erstwhile owners.

By the end of the last ice age (10,000 years ago), people in Europe were clearly interested in appearance over and above function. Certain objects had symbolic rather than functional qualities—none more so than the many "Venus" figurines, which might have been good luck charms in the fertility stakes, or symbols of a belief in a fertility cult.

Strike up the band! Music was probably invented not long after people were invented.

EVERY HOME SHOULD HAVE ONE

Beat that drum

All human races and cultures enjoy music and have a sense of rhythm, and ritual music making must have provided a vital sort of cultural glue. Drums and rattles were probably the earliest instruments, but there is a debate as to whether the harp or the bow came first. Physically, they are very similar objects: you can twang them both, but only one fires arrows. Ancient wind instruments have also been found, carved from hollow bones with finger holes that show that notes and scales have an ancient history.

5000 B.C. The Egyptians build dikes and canals for irrigation as lands bordering the River Nile begin to dry out.

3600 B.C. Southwest Asians discover bronze, the first metal hard enough to cut with.

3200 B.C. The earliest form of writing is invented by the Sumerians; they also pioneer the wheel and the lunar calendar.

5000~1600 B.C.

Putting Down Roots
Society settles and develops

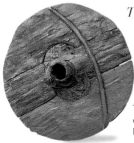

The plow: an invention that turned society on its head, because people began to plant seeds to grow crops. As early farming economies became more established, neolithic societies became more stable and less itinerant.

The invention that got everything moving, literally: the wheel.

This all seems to have begun c. 9000 B.C. in the Middle East, and over the next 3,000 years agriculture spread across Asia, arriving in Northern Europe from the Balkans around 1000 B.C. The Neolithics were home-boys and girls, and domestic culture grew. Neolithic farmers seem to have put down roots first around 6500 B.C., but plows took longer: probably they were in use around 3500 B.C.

They were just pieces of wood, but they really were revolutionary. Who needs a big green John Deere tractor to make a breakthrough? The Middle Eastern Neolithics cultivated more land, grew more crops, improved more soil, reduced famine, and (if the timing's right) got the story of Joseph into the bargain. Just spare a tear for

the Euro-Neolithics with their dismal wet weather: they had to wait another thousand years before that anonymous but heaven-sent guy invented an iron-bladed plow that could till their soggy soil. But they got there in the end.

DON'T JUST STAND THERE;
MAKE A CHAIR

In some ways, Neolithic design had a lot going for it, but if ever a society was to blame for the concept of A Woman's Place, this was it. Neolithic tools gave rise to small-scale industry. Without the Neolithics there would have been no tea parties: they were responsible for the potter's wheel, which was first used for "built" pottery in Mesopotamia around 3500 B.C.

This clay vessel dates from the second millennium B.C., and is the oldest known representation of a cart.

2640 B.C. Silk manufacture is introduced by the wife of the Chinese emperor Huang Ti.

c. 2575-2465 B.C. Pyramids are constructed at Giza on the banks of the Nile as gigantic memorials to the Egyptian pharaohs.

1700 B.C. A papyrus written during the reign of Re-Ser-Ka shows that Egyptians suffered from tooth decay and ophthalmic troubles.

EVERY HOME SHOULD HAVE ONE

The antler pick

It wasn't exactly the Swiss Army knife of its day, but an antler pick was easy to come by and the mainstay of many Neolithic toolkits, especially if you were a flint miner. Once you had the antler of a red deer, you bashed the bone until it was reduced to a picklike shape, and then—in an increasingly commercial world—you were in business.

Bronze was an easily molded material that lent itself to all kinds of tools.

And with bow lathes, they made furniture to sit on. The lathe was in use in the Middle East well before 3000 B.C., and it quickly caught on. It made those nice, spindly shapes that bowled the Egyptians over (just look at their copycat furniture), and the Greeks followed suit a little later.

While we're thinking about the same period, you can ditch any preconceived notions you may have concerning leather jackets: yes, the Neos got there first. Of course, no self-respecting 1960s biker would touch Neolithic leathers (at least not without the right insignia and some nice Gothic lettering), but they were durable and weatherproof. And probably very smelly, too.

THE AGE OF BRONZE

If the Neolithics didn't invent money, they were certainly among the first cultures to exchange copper coinage, though we don't know what value it had, or whether it was used instead of or in addition to bartering. Forget copper, though, and dig the new stuff, bronze, discovered by accident when someone smelted copper with tin ore, c. 3500 B.C. The new metal turned plowshares into swords and back again, and sculptors from Donatello to Henry Moore never looked back. Bronze was easier to work and more durable than copper, and well before 2000 B.C. the known world was happily blasting and casting.

LIVING BY NUMBERS

Some of the first numeral systems were devised well before Bible times. The Sumerians and Egyptians both evolved numbering processes that used Units, but those clever Chinese were the first to develop the Tens and Units that many of us used in elementary school. Each number from 1 to 10 had a special symbol, and then there was one for hundreds and thousands. In time, Hebrews and Greeks made refinements, and then the Romans (those confusing Cs, Xs, and Vs), until we finally settled for a hodgepodge of Arabic and Hindu symbols just before A.D. 1000. It took long enough, didn't it?

1520 B.C. A volcanic eruption on the Greek island of Thera (Santorini) destroys all life on the island.

1470 B.C. Mycenae is established as a new cultural center by survivors of the Minoan civilization destroyed in Crete.

c. 750 B.C. Homer writes the *Iliad* and the *Odyssey*.

1600 B.C.~A.D. 400

Sunny Prospects
Classical antiquity

Six thousand years ago, the roots of civilization were beginning to sprout. The settled farming cultures around the Mediterranean Sea began to develop a flourishing pattern of trade. Trade needs goods, and goods need designing. Other trappings of commercial society were needed, too: transportation, bookkeeping, writing instruments. Trade and religion became respectively the driving forces for change and the glue of society.

An elegantly painted terra-cotta jug from around the seventh century B.C.

About 5,000 years ago, the Egyptians founded one of the most remarkably stable and long-lasting cultures in history. It's amazing to think that even the Romans thought the Egyptians were ancient history. The treasure house of Tutankhamun's tomb (1350 B.C.) provides a stunning insight into the incredible design ability of the mature Egyptian culture. Jewelry, furniture, glass, cabinets, boxes, ceramics, weapons, regalia, and fire-lighters: in other words, everything you needed in this world and the next one.

By 1500 B.C. the Eastern Mediterranean was a hotbed of development as powerful mini-empires became established on Crete and Cyprus. A vast seaborne trade developed in food, wine, oil, pottery,

A gilded wooden statuette showing the Pharoah Tutankhamun.

jewelry, furniture, musical instruments, etc. The design of these changed gradually as changes in styles and fashions affected them, but much more slowly than today.

Keeping up with the Jones's probably goes back to time immemorial, but with the settlement of cities it gets

431 B.C. Greek physician Empedocles presents his theory of the body's four "humors"—blood, bile, black bile, and phlegm—a concept that dominates medical thinking for centuries.

A.D. 44 Vomitoriums are popular in Rome—eat too much, throw up, then go back for more.

A.D. 321 Emperor Constantine assigns convicts to grind Rome's flour in an effort to hold back the rising price of food in an empire whose population has dwindled as a result of plague.

serious. You displayed your status through your possessions. For an object to be precious, it needed to be made of valuable materials and have had many hours of labor lavished on it.

Everything was made by hand, but there was a degree of mass-production: archeologists found a cache of three-quarters of a million Roman nails (12 tons) at Inchtuthil fort, by Hadrian's Wall in Scotland—dumped when the Romans departed in A.D. 87—and amphorae for storing wine and oil were made in the hundreds of thousands.

Strike a light

Oil lamps, burning animal fat, date back to 6000 B.C., but by Roman times they had become elaborate bronze objects, often in the form of animals. A four-legged one in the shape of a dog has the flame coming from its mouth and the oil reservoir in its head.

prosperity, benefiting from a good climate and a slave-based economy, gave them the luxury of contemplating the meaning of life, geometry, philosophy, mathematics, ethics, and esthetics.

This last item became highly developed with the visually conscious Greeks. The Egyptians had been good at triangles, but there were a lot more shapes to sort out, and Plato set about defining the basic geometric forms, the Platonic solids. Math, art, and design overlap in the study of proportion—the relationships between the dimensions of an object—and the Greeks pioneered it, discovering the Golden Section. This is represented by a rectangle in the ratio of 1:1.612, which is the proportion used in the front elevation of the Parthenon (completed in 436 B.C.).

The most recognizable design achievements of the Greeks are their decorated pottery, architecture, and the refinement of the alphabet into characters that come down to the present day.

```
━━━━━ EVERY HOME SHOULD HAVE ONE ━━━━━
```

Bricks

In dry climates the sun-dried brick provided a convenient and versatile method for constructing walls. From Sumerian times (2800 B.C.) they were cheap and easy to make from a local material—mud. Straw was added to reduce crumbling. The earliest were formed by hand, but by the time Jericho needed walls they were made in wooden molds.

GREECE: THE EVOLUTION OF IDEAS

After the volcanic eruption on Santorini destroyed the Cretan empire around 1450 B.C., other empires —Babylonian, Assyrian, and Phoenician—rose, each more sophisticated than the last in terms of their technology, craft and design, and trading skills. By the time of the rise of Greek culture, their

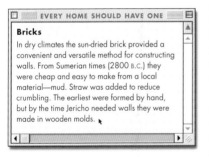

A decorated ceramic vessel from Greece showing men plowing with an ox (and a plow).

410 The Huns replace togas with slacks, making it easier to ride horses.

622 Mohammed travels from Mecca to Medina, a journey known as the Hegira, and Islam is founded.

900 England receives its first shipments of East Indian spices, used chiefly for medicinal purposes.

400~1800

Time Ticks By
Clocks

Tick tick tick tick … ka-boooom. The first major civilization with any time on its hands was that of the ancient Egyptians, who invented a form of shadow clock, rather like the (only slightly more modern) sundial, and also instituted the 24-hour day, irrespective of the season. When the Egyptians couldn't see the sun (at night, or during the Ninth Plague, when everything stood still), they used a water clock: makes you feel funny, doesn't it?

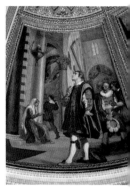

Galileo contemplates the principle of the pendulum.

BELOW: Spherical pointer from a monumental Roman sun calendar, begun c. 13 B.C.

Sundials were accurate enough but impractical (especially if you lived somewhere like Scotland, where the sun doesn't come out much). However, they were a timekeeper's mainstay throughout the Middle Ages until the eighteenth century. That's when the word "clock" was first heard, from the German *Glocke*, which means "bell": you could hear 'em long before you could see 'em, because no one had had the sense to design a clock face at that time.

For renascent individuals who couldn't stand the pace, portable clocks were available from c.1400. And if you really needed to know the time, and a policeman wasn't around, a well-designed chronometer might be yours in preference to an hourglass—a great invention, ideal

---

EVERY HOME SHOULD HAVE ONE

Atomic!

The first atomic clock was built in Washington, D.C., in 1948, following designs by Dr. Willard Frank Libby, and another followed in 1955, built in Teddington, near London, England. They worked by counting the natural atomic oscillations of cesium and ammonia, and were accurate to within 1 second in 300 years. Like most modern computers, the size of atomic clocks has decreased dramatically, from large models weighing hundreds of pounds to objects capable of fitting into a grocery box.

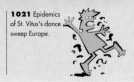
1021 Epidemics of St. Vitus's dance sweep Europe.

1450 Flatware (rather than fingers) begins to be accepted as the eating equipment of choice for the gentry.

1762 Voltaire (François-Marie Arouet 1694–1778) publishes *Candide*, a satire on materialism, politics, greed, and guile.

on ships and the ultimate naval clock until the 1600s: the British Royal Navy kept theirs rolling and tumbling until 1820. In 1761 the RN received an unusual invention in the shape of Harrison's Marine Chronometer, built after a strangled plea from the British Parliament, since the navy desperately needed to discover longitude because (a) latitude was lonely on its own, and (b) (can you believe this?) ships were floundering all over the place, getting lost and losing trade.

But let's face it: these machines weren't the beginnings of the watch. These small clocks were first made in Germany (Nuremberg, so it's said) around 1500. It's also said that *Leonardo da VINCI* (1452–1519) drew one, c.1490. You could

Wicked!

There is an old English myth about King Alfred (scourge of the Danes) inventing a method of time measurement using candles. You marked them, they melted, and time passed by. Simple, but inaccurate! It might have been true—but it's not likely. Either way, candles were certainly around, made from strands of flax inserted into collected animal fat and designed to give light and to offer a measure of time, from around 2000 B.C.

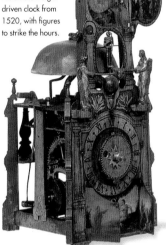
An ornate weight-driven clock from 1520, with figures to strike the hours.

carry a watch in your pocket because it had spiral springs, which allowed it to function anywhere.

Then there were pendulum clocks (c.1656), which combined Galileo's experiments with designs by the Dutchman *Christiaan HUYGENS* (1629–93). The first pendulum clock was accurate to about five minutes a day—not bad at all when you're waiting for a friend—and was the best on the market for nearly 200 years. Then in 1840 the scientist Bain's electromagnetic clock appeared, and when it was plugged into the outlet…well, joy just sparked, unfettered, and Life became enslaved to Time. Forever.

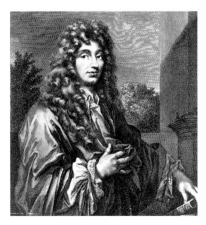
Dutch astronomer Christiaan Huygens, creator of the first pendulum clock and also the discoverer of Saturn's rings.

1203 A large brewing industry develops at Hamburg and in the Lowlands as barley malt from the Baltic becomes more readily available at lower prices.

1233 The Japanese royal family adopts the ancient custom of *ohaguro* (staining teeth black) as a sign of beauty.

1275 Marco Polo arrives at the court of Kublai Khan in Shan-tu, China; his detailed memoirs of his visit will be a bestseller for several centuries.

1200~1450

Goth, That'th Gorgeouth!
Seminal developments in the Middle Ages

Banqueting in style chez le Duc de Berry: an illustration from a book of hours.

If you ask someone what was designed in this period, they might come up with cathedrals, but not much else. However, these were interesting times—if you survived beyond childhood, and avoided the plague like the plague. The pace of change was sedate, but slowly the Dark Age blues wore off.

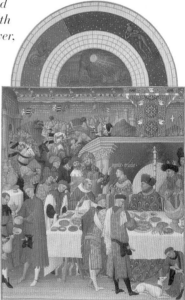

The Gothic arch was an important structural advance, and the style it symbolized was the first international design fad. It was to influence architecture for centuries to come, with frequent revivals up to the present day.

This was a time when "designer" was an unknown term. Anyone who had done an apprenticeship could turn a hand to design. Painters and craftsmen (and craftswomen) doubled as tapestry, glass, book, and jewelry designers. The rich, of whom there were few, were fabulously rich. Such a person was the Duc de Berry, who commissioned incredible objects from the finest artist-designers of the period. The poor, of whom there were many, were grovelingly poor, but even they needed a few basic household utensils, "designed" and made by the local craftsmen—pots, cudgels, crude furniture based on existing patterns.

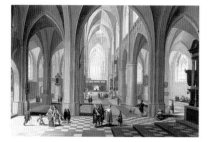

The most visible legacy of the Middle Ages: a Gothic cathedral interior.

1315 The first public systematic dissection of a human body is supervised by Italian surgeon Mondino de Luzzi.

1390 The *Forme of Cury* is an early cookbook of recipes served to Richard II and his barons. It includes a recipe for Italian macaroni.

1454 French musicians perform inside a huge pie at the Feast of the Pheasant for the Duke of Burgundy: they are commemorated in the nursery rhyme "Sing a Song of Sixpence."

Don't try this at home.
Gunpowder isn't really a "design," more a recipe, but its discovery led to the design of many devices that were mainly concerned with killing people.

Gunpowder, also known as "black powder," is a combination of sulfur, charcoal, and potassium nitrate. Grind up the damp ingredients in the correct proportion, compress and dry. Because it explodes relatively slowly, it is also an ideal propellant, and the Chinese quickly realized the possibility of rockets. This led in due course to the Moon landing of 1969—but also to firework displays, one of the most ephemeral forms of design in existence.

The first pocket watch (German, of course), made in Nuremberg in 1510.

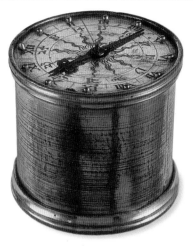

AGENTS OF CHANGE

Why don't we still live in feudal serfdom? Because of change, brought about by our less noble qualities. Greed motivated exploration and warfare. The conquest of distant lands was the way to add to your riches. The need for accurate navigation led to more reliable maps, and better timekeeping and astronomical observation. The feudal world that dominated the so-called dark ages gradually gave way as the power of merchants increased and trade became as important as militarism for survival. There is also the "comfort factor"; some historians think we progressed (i.e., invented central heating) because it made us more comfortable.

In these dark days, two important inventions arrived in Europe from the Far East. One, peaceful and useful, was paper. The other, very destructive but also useful, was gunpowder. Paper transformed the transmission of ideas when it got together with printing *(see page 22)*. Gunpowder was the origin of a permanent competition to have the most deadly weapons.

Design has been much affected by war— we have become adept at designing things that kill people. At that time, however, the Black Death was more efficient than any weapons, and took no prisoners.

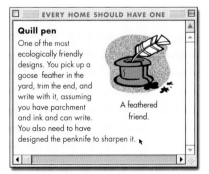

EVERY HOME SHOULD HAVE ONE

Quill pen
One of the most ecologically friendly designs. You pick up a goose feather in the yard, trim the end, and write with it, assuming you have parchment and ink and can write. You also need to have designed the penknife to sharpen it.

A feathered friend.

1475 The world's first coffee house opens at Constantinople, under the name Kiva Han.

1544 Northern Europe suffers a honey shortage as a result of the breakup of monasteries by the Reformation.

1560 A smallpox epidemic decimates Portugal's Brazilian colony and increases the need for African slaves to cut sugarcane.

1450~1650

Moving Type, Fixed Stars
Renaissance developments

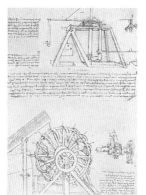

Johannes Gutenberg, without whom you would not be reading this book.

Having escaped from the privations of the medieval era, the Europeans could now concentrate on designing a new world. Centered on Italy, the Humanist movement rediscovered Classical (i.e., Roman and Greek) principles of taste in all aspects of culture: architecture, sculpture, science, literature, and philosophy.

With clever timing, one *Johannes Gutenberg* of Mainz, Germany (1394–1469), perfected a method of printing with movable type. He had the brilliant idea of mass-producing books that looked like the familiar ones scribes had written. Printing was one of the first examples of making lots of identical copies of the same thing—i.e., mass production, the basis of consumerism. Unfortunately, he went bust before he turned in a profit, but the concept quickly caught on, and printing spread rapidly across Europe. Fortunately for us, Venetian publishers adopted a revivalist "Roman" typeface, as opposed to the "Gothic" scribe style then popular in Germany. The invention of printing combined with a thirst for knowledge and led to cheaper books.

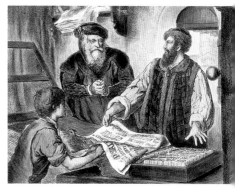

Incredible power and wealth enabled Italian families like the Medicis to sponsor every aspect of design from tableware to castles. Leonardo da Vinci is renowned as one of the most inventive minds of the period, but sadly his genius had little direct impact in his time—his

Some drawings by Leonardo the designer-inventor, well ahead of his times.

1588 The Spanish Armada is defeated in the English Channel by Sir Francis Drake's British fleet.

1626 Sir Francis Bacon experiments with the idea of freezing chickens by stuffing them with snow; he catches pneumonia and dies.

1637 René Descartes publishes *A Discourse on Method*, applying scientific rigor to the understanding of the human mind.

notebooks were eagerly filched away into private libraries and never widely seen. They could have been, for the illustrated encyclopedia emerged at the same time (the *Nuremberg Chronicle*, 1493), but Leonardo missed the boat, or rather the book. Most of his designs had to wait 200 years to be reinvented.

EVERY HOME SHOULD HAVE ONE

The fork

Somehow we had managed for several thousands of years without forks: eating with just a knife and fingers was good enough even for royalty, but from 1463 we have a record of an English gentleman using a fork to eat green ginger. Table manners never looked back.

Trade secrets

In an age before factories, the importance of craftspeople as the providers of goods was central—and they knew it. Skill and techniques were jealously guarded, and craft guilds preserved their secrets. Only by purchasing a long apprenticeship could you get in on the act, and you would probably need a relative in the trade already.

THE SKY: NO LONGER THE LIMIT

New technologies and materials stimulated the design of new objects. Early optical devices seemed like magic: a tube with some bits of glass in each end that would make things look nearer, and a similar one that made tiny things visible. The aim of the emergent sciences was to understand how nature worked, but this in turn led to making *things* that worked. Galileo improved the design of Dutch telescopes and revealed new wonders in the sky. This was a period of expansion and progress, with conditions that favored free enterprise and invention.

Nuremberg at the time of the famous *Chronicle*, 1493.

1702 England's Queen Anne gives royal approval to horseracing, and sweepstakes for cash prizes begin.

1707 A pulse watch invented by English physician John Floyer, designed to run for exactly one minute, is the first efficient clinical precision instrument for medical diagnosis.

1712 French missionary Père d'Entrecolles sends back the first accurate description of how the Chinese make porcelain.

1650~1780

From Wood to Coal
The foundations of the industrial age

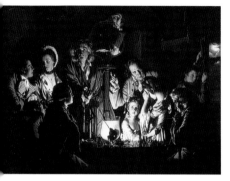

Life expectancy dipped in the seventeenth century all across Europe as wars, pestilence, and plague took their toll. And yet there was a sense of progress and change, which centered on the gradual shift to a more industrial scale of energy-generation.

Experiment with an Air Pump by Joseph Wright of Derby (1734–97). Shame about the bird.

Water, wind, and muscle were the forces that had driven the Old World. Machines were known—windmills and winches on a large scale, clocks and watches on a small scale—but they were still relatively rare. For centuries wood had been a primary material for practically everything, including heating, and it was beginning to run out. Forests were cut down to meet the demand for building, furniture, and ships—and also for charcoal, essential for smelting iron.

To counter the shortage of wood, its fossil fuel was increasingly exploited: coal. Gradually, mining became more important. But as mines got deeper, they were inclined to flood, and hand pumps were laborious and inefficient. *Thomas SAVERY's* (c. 1650–1715)

very primitive steam pump of 1698 was the first, soon outmoded by *Thomas NEWCOMEN's* (1663–1729) design for a coal-powered engine, the first successful one in the world, which started working in 1712 with the unimagined power of five horses, day and night! The steam age had started; life would never be the same again.

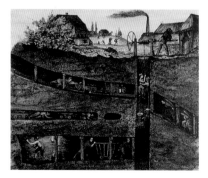

Industrial ants: coal mining in the nineteenth century, with child labor.

1721 Broccoli arrives in England around 70 years after the so-named Italian asparagus became popular in France.

1733 Smugglers evade Britain's new Molasses Act by transporting African slaves to Spanish colonies, trading them for molasses and sugar, and selling the cargo to New England distillers.

1739 Persia's Nadir Shah seizes the 109-carat Koh-i-noor diamond in the sack of Delhi. The diamond is later acquired by the East India Company and presented to Queen Victoria in 1850.

SCIENCE AND THE CITY

The changes of this period, especially those involving the use of machines, led to the Industrial Revolution. This was in part due to the accumulation of knowledge since the Renaissance. Now a rush of crucial inventions—which were designs as much as they were inventions—changed the way people lived and how they were to earn a living.

From now on there would be a steady drift of population from the countryside to the city. This in turn broke the mold of the social system that had dominated village life. Less visible inventions such as banking and capitalism also encouraged change and growth. (The first paper money was introduced in Sweden in 1661.) These concepts merged into a belief in progress, that there were better ways of doing things. By the middle of the eighteenth century, the first pioneering changes were evident: *John KAY's* (1704–78) flying shuttle revolutionized weaving, *Jethro TULL's* (1674–1740) seed drill improved agriculture, and the blast furnace was to make iron widely available.

Watt's the story?

James Watt (1736–1819) was a skilled instrument maker, and his fame is centered on the vast improvements he made to the efficiency and power of steam engines. He perfected his own design in 1769. By 1800 there were 500 Watt engines at work in England, underpinning the Industrial Revolution. He also designed the "governor," the first feedback device for regulating machines.

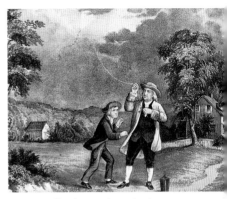

Benjamin Franklin taking his life in his hands: the famous thunderstorm experiment, c. 1746.

DESIGNER NAMES

Some designs seem slight and incidental (the "I could have thought of that" type), yet have a profound effect on everyday life—none more so than the lightning rod, which **Benjamin Franklin** *(1706–90) devised following his dangerous experiment with kites in thunderstorms.*

With all that wood around, fire was a major hazard of the time. The Great Fire of London (1666) had destroyed the medieval city, opening the way to the grand designs of Christopher Wren's new buildings.

A genuine all-rounder, Franklin was also responsible for the design of the greatly improved cast-iron stove that still bears his name.

DESIGNER NAMES

1750 London's Westminster Bridge opens and becomes the first new bridge to span the Thames since London Bridge in the tenth century.

1759 Irish brewer Arthur Guinness establishes a brewery in Dublin that subsequently becomes the largest in the world.

1762 English potter Josiah Wedgwood is appointed "Potter to the Queen."

1750~1800

Doing the Dishes
Wedgwood pottery

What Josiah WEDGWOOD (1730–95) didn't quite manage to do himself, he had others do for him. He put Staffordshire pottery on the map, became a mega-contributor to the Industrial Revolution, and gave the Art Boys jobs. To finish his ceramic designs, he engaged some of the very best artists of the day: John FLAXMAN (1755–1826), horse whisperer George STUBBS (1724–1806), and from just down the road, Joseph WRIGHT "of Derby" (1734–97).

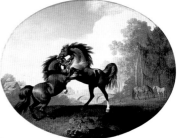

Stallions Fighting by George Stubbs: vivid detail from a piece of Wedgwood biscuitware.

Imagine we're in the 1760s. Neo-classicism is becoming the order of the day, and it's going to stay that way for quite a while. In fashion and design, ancient Greece and Rome are back in vogue; all is slender and graceful. The Adam brothers are just around the corner (and over the page).

Wedgwood isn't a designer; he's an entrepreneur. He needs skilled artists to finish ceramics turned out using mechanical devices, like lathes.

Queen's Ware, Wedgwood's old-age pension, from an 1870 pattern book.

He's got his employees continually experimenting, making ceramics that he divides into two categories: "ornamental" and "useful." He's more organized than Birmingham-based rival *Matthew BOULTON* (1728–1809), who can't decide whether to make toys like his dad or head for the China clay business. Wedgwood's "ornamental" stuff, which is what we know best, wouldn't have been possible without the "useful" ware. Wedgwood's great ceramic triumph was "Queen's Ware," which arrived in 1763 and went straight onto the dining room table, no question.

Gardez-Loo

What's in a name? The head, privy, john, potty, or WC came into its own in 1775, when the first pot worth the name was invented by Alexander Cummings, by day a watchmaker in London's prestigious Bond Street. The bowl or pan was metal. You pulled up a handle and activated a valve, an overhead tank released water, and presto: the nasty stuff was flushed into a cess-pit. This arrangement was improved three years later by another Londoner, Joseph Bramah, who went so far as to patent his invention. In the long term it caused a stink: London's sewerage system had to be re-designed after a Royal Commission was appointed by the then Prime Minister, Benjamin Disraeli.

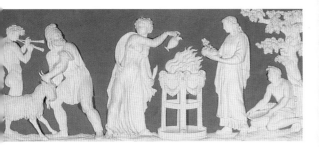

It was cheap earthenware, it looked great, and it was easily made, using production-line methods, with different patterns. J.W. understood market forces well. By 1773 he had printed six editions of his catalog *Useful Ware*. Hotcakes? You bet. He was an eighteenth-century success story who tried hard to balance the needs of a snobbish clientele—who wanted novelty—with the durability and usefulness required by the less wealthy.

It was an absorbing problem. His clients wanted to impress their friends, but Wedgwood wanted to make money. It wasn't always easy to achieve a happy medium, combining the "useful" with the "ornamental," or as he himself said,

This Bacchanalian scene by John Flaxman is typical of the eighteenth-century taste for all things neoclassical.

"elegance and simplicity." In fact, some of his shapes were actually…um… rather ugly. A cauliflower-shaped coffee pot, madam? Yes? Well, there's no accounting for taste…

Wedgwood's Staffordshire factory, "Etruria," in 1769.

EVERY HOME SHOULD HAVE ONE

Wedgwood miniatures

Twentieth-century Wedgwood somehow just isn't quite right. Go for something smaller and earlier—perhaps a Wedgwood brooch or miniature with a sense of history. You can pass it on to your kids without having to worry about maintenance, and it still has a feel of real quality behind it, because it was first made for people who cared about Things.

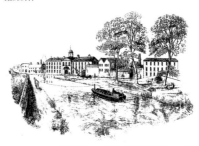

1762 New York's first St. Patrick's Day parade on March 17 celebrates a man historians will agree was not named Patrick, not Irish, did not bring Christianity to, nor drive snakes from, Ireland, and was not born on March 17.

1788 The first penal colonies are established in Botany Bay in Australia as a dumping ground for English criminals.

1790 U.S. Congress establishes a patent office to protect inventors and give them an incentive to develop new machines and methods.

1750~1820

Pillars of Society
The Brothers Adam

In the heady neoclassical world of fluted columns, pilasters, and well-turned chair legs Robert (1728–92) and James (1732–94) ADAM were Britain's first international style bandits.

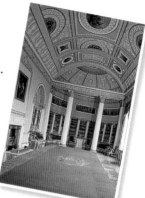

Megastars, they peddled enough ideas robbed from the Antique in architecture and design to make your eyes pop out. And that boring little squirt Robert (yes, he really was) ended up as Big Boss Man.

The library at Kenwood House, on London's Hampstead Heath.

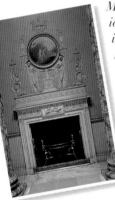

Robert Adam fireplace at Kedleston Hall, a Derbyshire dream house in pale pastels, c. 1760.

Grand-touring in Italy in 1755–57, young Roberto learned (a) all about the styles of the ancient past, in depth; (b) how to draw properly; (c) how to draw decor properly; (d) how to make friends and influence people properly; and (e) how to impress English (but aristocratic) grand tourists with his own "new" decor based on the classical Antique.

Robbie broke his homeward journey to draw Diocletian's palace at Spalatro (now Split). Back in Britain, he began hawking his new Classical style to the gentry. Like it or loathe it (and there were lots of

loathers), the Adams altered the British landscape. Kedleston Hall (Derbyshire, 1760–61), Syon House (Middlesex, 1760–69), and Kenwood (Hampstead, 1767–69) are three of their Greatest Hits. All display the Adam brothers' belief in "total" (not their word) interior decor, from paintwork to metalwork.

Grandeur (but no central heating) at Syon House, Middlesex.

1793 French revolutionaries turn the Tuileries gardens in Paris into a potato field. A French ordinance forbids consumption of more than one pound of meat per week on pain of death.

1803 Morphine is discovered by German pharmacist Friedrich Wilhelm Adam Saturner, who names it after of the Greek god of dreams, Morpheus.

1819 French physician René Théophile Hyacinthe Laënnec invents the stethoscope, using a roll of paper to avoid the indelicacy of placing his ear to the bosom of a female patient.

But perhaps the brothers' greatest claim to fame was their *Works in Architecture of Robert and James Adam* (1773, 1779, 1822). This book went to three volumes, the first being the best known because it persuasively promoted what the boys called the "Etruscan" style. It wasn't, of course, but it was hip, with its pale, pastel paint and classical motifs. To support it, plasterers, carpet manufacturers, and silversmiths were all intellectually mugged, among them—perhaps most famously—the great cabinetmaker *Thomas Chippendale* (1718–79), furniture-führer to the gentry. Chippendale's designs were rarely brilliant, but always competent and sound. Aside from other commissions, he often worked on Adam projects (but to his own designs) during the 1760s, and—unlike Bob and Jim—seems wisely not to have risked his reputation or career.

DESIGNER NAMES

Sure, the Adamses altered the face of British architectural design and decor. But Robert owed much of his success to **Charles-Louis Clerriseau** *(1721–1820), whom he engaged as his drawing master, and also to famed etcher and antiquarian* **Giovanni Battista Piranesi** *(1720–78). Typically, neither were fully credited for their efforts.*

financial intervention of their dull but canny brother John. A close shave, which no amount of chutzpah could disguise.

The inspiration of the Antique: an "Etruscan style" chair by Georges Jacob (1739–1814), Versailles.

EVERY HOME SHOULD HAVE ONE

An Adam fireplace

Most Adam houses have several. One of their great houses must have something to your taste, in marble or alabaster, with a Greco-Roman pattern, or perhaps one of their famous "Etruscan" designs: your friends will be lost for words when they see yours. But please: no imitations. They're so...tacky.

The Adam boys hit the skids with a speculative scheme for palatial apartments at the Adelphi (1768–72), on the north bank of the River Thames. No one wanted to buy the horrid little boxes, and R and J's hides were saved only by a lottery and the

1811 The Russian ambassador to Paris, Prince Aleksandr Borosovich Kurakin, introduces the practice of serving meals in courses instead of placing all the dishes on the table at once.

1820 At the age of 40, English Quaker minister Elizabeth Gurney marries chocolate heir Joseph Fry and works to improve conditions in English prisons.

1839 In Canton, Lin Tse-hsu confiscates some opium warehouses belonging to British traders, and the First Opium War begins.

1800~1900

Sitting Pretty
Chairs

A simple rustic seat.

Chairs have been around for as long as we have needed to take the weight off our feet. First they were boulders and then tree trunks, but at some distant time someone crafted the first chair, or (more likely) stool. Lowly people had stools—think of milkmaids—while at the other end of the scale feudal lords and bishops, and of course kings and queens, had chairs (or thrones) appropriate to their status. Hundreds of years later, chairs can still perform that socially defining role.

A nineteenth-century papier-mâché chair with cane seat and mother-of-pearl.

A history of chairs from ancient Egypt to the nineteenth century is really the history of carpentry. The transformation of wood from raw planks to elegant, sophisticated, and subtle shapes is a tribute to the skills of craftsmen who have continuously handed down and improved their techniques over many centuries.

Other factors, too, have changed the look of chairs. The importation of exotic woods from the tropics in the eighteenth century coincided with a desire for more elegant furniture, and *Thomas* SHERATON (1751–1806), *Thomas* CHIPPENDALE (1718–79), and *George* HEPPLEWHITE (d. 1786) were on hand to provide the goods. All three also published or

contributed to influential books, such as Chippendale's *The Gentleman and Cabinet Maker's Director* (1754), which was in effect a trade catalog. Drawing on fashionable fads, you could take your pick from Gothic, Chinese, and modern designs. "Modern" at that time meant rococo, the international, florid, and highly ornamental style that affected painting, architecture, and interior design.

A Hepplewhite dining chair, c. 1750. They don't make them like that any more.

1853 The first U.S. world's fair opens at New York in the Crystal Palace Exposition, modeled on the 1851 Great Exhibition in London.

1876 In the U.S., foil-wrapped bananas fetch 10¢ each at the Philadelphia fair, giving most fairgoers their first taste of tropical fruit.

1891 Carnegie Hall opens on West 57th Street, New York, built with $2 million donated by steel magnate Andrew Carnegie.

NEW WAYS, NEW SHAPES

Experimentation was in the air in the early nineteenth century. In America *Samuel Gragg* (1772–1855) of Boston created original chair designs by exploiting the best qualities of three woods, steaming and bending them into elegant shapes. Twenty years later in Austria, a similar idea was being tried out by *Michael Thonet* (1796–1871). By 1842 he had perfected a method of bending strips of laminated beechwood into curlicue shapes. In 1858 he designed the No. 14 chair, a sensationally simple concept, made from five component parts that could be mass-produced and packed flat. This was the café chair of the world and was to be made in its millions, right up to the present day—the VW of chairs.

> **EVERY HOME SHOULD HAVE ONE**
>
> ### A piano
> What could be a more respectable possession to show you were a cultured prosperous person than to have a piano in the home? Originating in Italy in the early eighteenth century, the piano as object spread rapidly through Europe, and by 1783 John Broadwood of London had added foot-pedals to it.

Michael Thonet's No. 14 chair, a prizewinner if ever there was one.

Cast iron was the material the Victorians excelled in, and they used it to create the first patio and conservatory furniture. Another novel material of the period was based on papier mâché, but not as we know it. By pressing paper with glue under great pressure, rigid forms could be molded, including whole chairs. These were precursors of the curved shapes of plastic chairs that appeared a hundred years later.

To make this substance acceptable in the home, the furniture was inlaid with mother-of-pearl and black-lacquered to imitate the Chinese look. This idea was later copied by Singer to make the sewing machine less conspicuous.

1827 English astronomer Frederick William Herschel invents contact lenses.

1828 The Zoological Gardens in Regent's Park, London, open to the public, featuring the first hippo to be seen in Europe since the ancient Romans showed one at the Colosseum.

1833 Chicago carpenter Augustus Deodat Taylor revolutionizes housing construction in the U.S. with his simple-to-construct and sturdy balloon frame.

1820~1850

Smile, Please
The invention of the camera

As the Victorian age settled down to affluence and middle-class comforts, it needed distractions. What could be more intriguing than a device that stopped nature in its tracks? The Victorians were keen on the idea of conquering "nature"; it made them feel all-powerful, and as Britain had an empire on which the sun never set, they already had the right mindset.

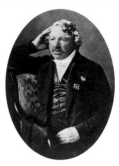

Louis Daguerre, pioneer photographer, c. 1850.

Artists who were frustrated by their inability to draw well had long resorted to an aid called the camera obscura (literally, "dark room"), which enabled them to sketch over a picture projected through a lens. The painter Canaletto had made great use of it. Many had thought how brilliant it would be if one could "capture" these projected images, and advances in chemistry made this possible by the 1830s. By remarkable coincidence, two inventor-designers quite independently pulled off the trick at the same time, but with two different processes. They were to change the way we saw

Picture in a box: a Daguerre camera made by Giroux, 1839.

ourselves and the world, and add to the sense of the visual that is so much a part of our culture today.

Louis Daguerre (1789–1851), in France, and *William Henry Fox Talbot* (1800–77), in England, designed the first cameras. Mrs. Fox Talbot called them "mouse traps" because this is what they looked like. It is often the case that a new invention follows the form of an existing one—think of the horseless carriage.

Read all about it
Before photographs could be printed, wood engravings were the medium for pictures. Two of the pioneer publishers were *Punch*, a satirical magazine in 1841, and *The Illustrated London News* in 1842. Both were widely read and reflected Victorian tastes and interests.

1841 Scottish surgeon James Baird discovers hypnosis.

1845 Two million Irish people die or emigrate during the Great Famine.

1849 The bowler hat (derby) is created by London hatmakers Thomas Bowler, Ltd, who made the hat to order for customer William Coke, who wanted protection from overhanging branches while out shooting.

The impact of the daguerreotype was rapid, and Daguerre generously didn't patent the process. By the 1850s there were hundreds of daguerreotype studios throughout the world, with everyone lining up to have their portraits "taken." All but the very poor could now have a portrait for the parlor wall. Each daguerreotype was a unique one-off on a copper plate, but Fox Talbot's process, rapidly improved upon, allowed for multiple prints, and later enlargements. In 1844 Fox Talbot published the first book to be illustrated with photographs, *The Pencil of Nature*.

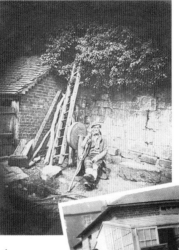

Fox Talbot took the photographic process a stage further by using silver chloride paper. This is his *Man with a Crutch* from 1844.

Fox Talbot at work. Special measures were used to keep the sitter's head still during the long exposure needed for the photograph.

DESIGNER NAMES

At much the same time as the camera was being invented, the British self-taught scientist **Michael Faraday** (1791–1867) devised the first electric motor in 1821. Although only a toy, as Hero's steam engine had been centuries before, its development was to have one of the most profound effects on how we live our lives. Faraday went on to design the first machine to "make" electricity from mechanical energy, by rotating a wire around a magnet, in 1831. This was the foundation of all subsequent electrical supply. Faraday went on to become Director of the Royal Institution.

In the very same year, **Joseph Henry** (1797–1878) in the U.S. perfected his electromagnetic motor. These two concepts, and the wires in between, provide the basis of our electric world. Can you imagine life without the vacuum cleaner and the hairdryer?

DESIGNER NAMES

1827 New Orleans has its first Mardi Gras celebration in February, an event introduced by Parisian students to mark Shrove Tuesday.

1831 Chloroform is invented independently by German chemist Justus von Liebig and U.S. pharmacist Samuel Guthrie.

1835 The *New York Herald* begins publication and is directed from its cellar office by Scottish-American journalist James Gordon Bennett with only two wooden chairs, an old dry-goods box, and $500.

1820~1900

Getting into Practice
European design

When is an art school not an art school? When it's a design school, of course. In nineteenth-century Britain, separating Design from Art was a knotty problem, bitterly debated by many eminent Victorians. Much revolved around life drawing (yes, nudes!), and whether or not to agree that it was a suitable subject for young trainee draftspeople. What had gone wrong?

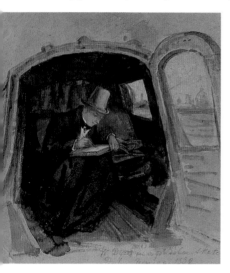

Watercolor by David Scott showing William Dyce sketching in Venice from a gondola, 1832.

Having kick-started the Industrial Revolution, the British had let go of the reins, and knew it. Clever continentals were getting fat on British mass-production methods, and even exhibiting the results, and Westminster was definitely unhappy.

How could the British grab back some of the action? Let's see…set up vocational schools of design to ape your Continental neighbors, and presto! In 1837, amid a great hullabaloo, a London School of Design (later the Royal College of Art) is finally established, and the dour Scottish painter *William Dyce* (1806–64) sniffs his way through Europe on an official fact-finding mission to discover where industrial design techniques are taught best. Dyce likes France, but *loves* Prussia, Bavaria, and Saxony, and so the German ideas are enshrined within new branch Schools of Design set up throughout Britain in the early 1840s.

Result? British design students begin to draw, but not interesting or useful things. Oh, no. Boring, repetitive stuff, in the interests of perfecting certain shapes. Ornaments, ironwork, textiles, ceramics, furniture. All very laudable, but…

1846 Swedish preacher Eric Janson founds Bishop Hill, 100 miles west of Chicago, and predicts an imminent apocalypse.

1861 The song lyrics "Maryland! My Maryland!" by James R. Randall are set to the music of the German Christmas song "O Tannenbaum."

1886 The first tuxedo dinner jacket is worn by American tobacco heir Griswold Lorillard, to the Autumn Ball of the Tuxedo Park Country Club at Tuxedo, New York.

At this stage, the absence of life drawing from design education is beginning to upset a lot of very influential people. Plus, no one's teaching about color, or form…the acrimony is contagious, and lasts until the end of the century, when the British Schools of Design are forced to develop into Schools of Art and Design, unified under a single teaching system controlled from London's South Kensington, home to the Victoria and Albert Museum, with its collection of "good" design.

But what *is* good design? Dyce is no more, and the Germans are doing it for themselves. The Berlin Decorative Arts and Design Museum is a leader in its field. Founded in 1867 as a private collection, by 1879 its collections are truly

> ☐ ▬▬ EVERY HOME SHOULD HAVE ONE ▬▬ ▤
>
> **Victorian figure drawing**
> A good example of Victorian life drawing will go well on one of your walls. True, it'll date from quite late, but real effort will have gone into it, because some poor student (if you can discover the author, it might be worth more) had to sweat to get it right.

encyclopedic, and by 1900 they include examples of contemporary design from every part of the globe. Their artifacts are held up as shining examples for every future German designer…though agreement isn't universal on this score. Odd, how you can't please everyone, isn't it?

NAMES

To say that the history of America was written in blood is putting the cart before the horse, but it's true, and men like **Samuel Colt** *(1814–62) and* **Philo Remington** *(1816–89) gave design history a helping hand and turned the U.S. into a major industrial nation. In 1851 Sam showed just how many mass-produced Navy .36 revolvers could be made using interchangeable machined parts. By 1874 Philo showed that the same technology could be used to turn swords into plowshares after the*

Colt army revolver, 1892.

Civil War: he switched to making lots and lots of typewriters.

In the same twenty years, **Isaac Merritt Singer** *(1811–75) not only claimed to have invented the home sewing machine, but he, too, used the same technology to produce 10,000 of them. And to more the product he used a novel sales pitch—yes folks, credit, the scourge of the bourgeoisie.*

Singer "New Family" sewing machine, 1865.

1854 Europe has 14,000 miles of rail track, connecting most major cities.

1858 English dressmaker Charles Frederick Worth opens a Paris boutique and establishes the first house of haute couture.

1865 A British mountain-climbing party led by artist Edward Whymper makes the first ascent of the Matterhorn, but four unfortunate members fall to their deaths on the descent.

1850~1900

Greenhouse Effect
The Great Exhibition

When he wasn't being the famously adoring husband of Britain's Queen Victoria (a full-time job), PRINCE ALBERT OF SAXE-COBURG-GOTHA (1819–61) was a world-heavyweight design enthusiast. His status mostly came in handy. With one eye firmly on developments in European industrial design and manufacture, and as president of the Society of Arts, Albert helped to devise a London exhibition so large that it would be called A Great Exhibition of the Industry of All Nations (phew!), and it would be held in 1851, so there.

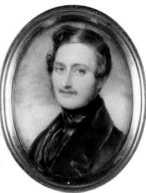

Good Prince Albert, miniaturized by William Charles Ross, c. 1840.

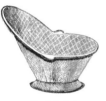

The tin bathtub, backbone of Victorian hygiene.

But me no buts, except…there was no building big enough to take it, and no one around to build one pretty enough. Enter architect, ex-gardener, and greenhouse builder to the Duke of Devonshire, *Joseph PAXTON* (1801–65). He was an unexpected entrant to the architectural contest, with a Cinderella's slipper of a building: a prefabricated glass and iron structure soon nicknamed (by *Punch* magazine) the Crystal Palace. In reality this was (you guessed?) a giant greenhouse, 1,800 feet long, and every bit of it factory-built, prefabricated for erection in Hyde Park, the first ever of its type.

Prince Albie's boys were headed by *Henry COLE* (1808–82), already an eminent Victorian in the world of design. Cole's committee had no difficulty shoe-horning a vast array of designed objects into the Crystal Palace: the Great Exhibition opened on May 1, 1851, and was a Great (and profit-making) Success.

Plant life

Flowers and leaves on wallpaper and carpets, fronds carved into chairs: it's called Naturalism. The Great Exhibition had cartloads of it, and many critics gave it the thumbs down, because by 1850 it was old hat. But the naturalist ideal endured; without it, the future—in the shape of John Ruskin, William Morris, and the Art Nouveau designers—would have been very different.

1870 American inventor William W. Lyman patents the first can opener with a cutting wheel that rolls around a can's rim.

1884 The first roller-coaster opens at Coney Island, NY, put up by former Indiana Sunday school teacher Lemarcus A. Thompson.

1893 A new fountain is erected at London's Piccadilly Circus as a memorial to the late Lord Shaftesbury, whose puritanical attitudes are distinctly counter to the choice of subject for the fountain, Eros.

EVERY HOME SHOULD HAVE ONE

Victorian ironwork

Some decorative ironwork rescued from a defunct Victorian rail station will be hard to find, but it will be a real piece of the past, cast aside by some clown who closed a perfectly good railroad deep in Britain's heartland. A seat. A roof girder. A pump. They certainly knew how to overproduce in those days, and it's a pity that there's so little left. Or you could go to Dallas and see the smaller re-creation of the Crystal Palace.

So what? Well, it clearly showed the gap between attitudes toward design in Europe (and here please include Britain) and the U.S. The Europeans still clung to Renaissance virtues of craftsmanship and detail, of putting an object—any object—on a pedestal and admiring its intrinsic esthetic qualities, putting usefulness second. American delegates at the Great Exhibition actively promoted the opposite idea: of mass-production as a way to offer better-made, simply designed artifacts to more people, and so (they hoped) improve the quality of life.

NOT JUST A PRETTY PAIR OF WHISKERS

History hasn't been kind to Prince Albert: foreign, and far from the Englishman's stereotypical view of himself: stiff upper lip and cold baths at dawn, what. But foremost among Albert's many strengths (he was also a concert-quality musician) was a huge interest in improvements in art and design, which forced the Brits to take stock of themselves and attempt real direction in such matters, especially in art and design education.

Paxton's huge Crystal Palace, pictured in its original home in Hyde Park, the River Thames in the background.

Build your own Crystal Palace

Commandeer Dad's greenhouse. Take out the glass carefully and send that nasty aluminum frame to the recycling plant. Find a foundry that hasn't had all its workers laid off: somewhere that does those horrid rustic lawn chairs will do. Ask them to make you some large cast-iron hoops, with plenty of ornate leafy decoration. Have it all delivered to your front lawn and annoy the neighbors while the hoops fall over as you try to work out how to refit the glass.

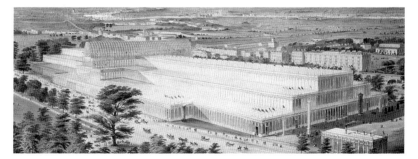

1800~1960

Write On

Fountain pens to fiber tips

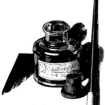

Pen and ink: once on every desk, now the preserve of the calligrapher.

May the muse be with you…Even a PC printer needs ink, and a typewriter has its ribbon—but these are mere chaff, dear reader, before the pleasure of handwriting with a real fountain pen. And anyway, writer's cramp is curable, whereas repetitive strain injury is a twentieth-century curse. From the dawn of civilization, every writer trying to make his or her mark on parchment, vellum, or paper had the same problem: sharpened reeds, quills, pointed stones, and odd bits of metal litter the trash cans of time.

Do or dye
The range of writing implements presently available to humanoids means that somewhere there's something to suit YOU, even if other methods have failed. One of the more original ideas has been the fiber-tip pen, which uses dye instead of ink to make a finer line on paper. It's as delicate as Japanese handwriting, which is not especially surprising, because that's what Yukio Horie intended to imitate when he developed it in 1962.

But in 1803 *Bryan DONKIN* (1768–1855) gave English writers something they could get their teeth into: a stick, with a patent steel nib attached. Decades of gritty ink in clogged inkwells followed (woznt skool a drag?). When Lewis Edson Waterman presented the world with its first fountain pen in 1884, he struck a blow for writers worldwide.

The experience of evenly flowing ink didn't come cheap, though. The expense and precision build of even a basic capillary-action fountain pen meant that such gold-nibbed pleasures were mainly

A Waterman cartridge pen, 1953. Cartridges were—up to a point—the answer to blots and blotting paper.

For Adults Only, although by the 1960s nearly every Western adult used a Parker, Waterman, Sheaffer, or other brand, usually chosen for longevity and price. Mass-production introduced cheap (and often unreliable) versions for 1950s teenagers, resulting in the massed blotting of copybooks.

1916 James Joyce's controversial semi-autobiographical novel *Portrait of the Artist as a Young Man* is published in New York.

1928 Scottish bacteriologist Alexander Fleming at St. Mary's Hospital, London, proves the antibacterial properties of penicillin, thus launching an "antibiotic" revolution in medicine.

1948 Scrabble is copyrighted by Connecticut businessman James Brunot. A friend had invented the game in 1931 and called it Criss-Cross.

EVERY HOME SHOULD HAVE ONE

A luxury pen

Good-quality fountain pens are wonderful objects, and will help you and yours to remember how to write well, and with feeling. A Mont Blanc would be very nice, thanks, but a good Waterman or Sheaffer will do just as well. And remember that pens are like cars: take a test write before purchase to make sure the little beauty fits snugly into your paw.

Inside, fountain pens haven't changed much from the messy ink-sucking plunger, lever, squeeze, or screw mechanisms of yesteryear (where are the tissues?), and "developments" like the disposable cartridge were (or are) merely alternative ink sources. And now? For the new, enhanced fountain pen, please thank the PC. Designers not only re-thought the materials used to make barrels and nib units, but also they used computer technology to change the ergonomics for the better (we have to hold the things, don't we?) and transformed a simple tool into a luxury item. Hey, we're talking about *writing* here. Remember writing?

Parker's "Big Red" Duofold, with its hard rubber barrel, made a colorful splash in 1922.

Throwaway roller-ball, the ubiquitous mainstay of offices everywhere.

ARE YOU READY TO ROLL?

Speaking from the other end of ostentation, it's now hard to imagine a time when ballpoint pens were frowned upon. But some teachers still hate them, because they ruin your handwriting (oh, they do). Ballpoints were on the drawing board in the nineteenth century, but the big breakthrough came in the 1930s when Hungarian *Ladislao* BIRÓ (1899–1985) made a prototype that had plenty of roll, but nothing like the pitch needed.

Eureka-time was mid-1940s, and no one has looked back. Dirt cheap. Hold it any-old-how. Constantly being improved. Students lose them all the time. Water-resistant ink but unresistant public and—as always—plenty of imitators. Under Marcel Bich, the French BIC company was first of many to jump on the bandwagon. There's someone's roller-writer near you now!

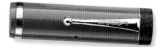

1830 Robert Livingston Stevens, son of steamboat pioneer John Stevens, invents the flanged T-rail, which will be the basis of future railroad track development.

1854 Lord Cardigan's name is given to the cardigan sweater; that of his commanding officer Field Marshal Fitzroy James Henry Somerset, Baron Raglan of Raglan, is given to the raglan-sleeve coat.

1863 President Lincoln proclaims the first national Thanksgiving Day and sets aside the last Thursday of November to commemorate the feast.

1830~1900

It's All About Communication
Typewriters and telephones

The bitterly fought American Civil War accelerated technical progress considerably, as war so often does. The need for large quantities of guns had led to the streamlining of manufacturing techniques in the U.S., far beyond anything in Europe. This was partly because the immigrant population was less hidebound by tradition, more eager to make their mark. It became known as the American system of manufacture.

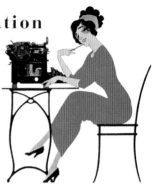

The happy typist, from a poster by Ernst Deutsch for Mercedes typewriters, c. 1911.

The conquest of the South by the North left the manufacturers, who had been enjoying fat contracts, without orders. Their shiny new machine tools, the most advanced in the world, had to make something. The Remington Small Arms Company had turned to agricultural tools, but then saw *Christopher SHOLES*'s (1819–90) typewriter, a startling new device, the result of five years' work perfecting a machine that made neat "printed-looking" text. Buying Sholes out, they launched the Remington No. 1 in 1876.

Although the public was slow to accept it, it was to revolutionize the office workplace. Before the typewriter, all office clerks were men. After it, they were increasingly women, for whom work prospects were dramatically changed. Similarly, the invention of the telephone by *Alexander Graham BELL* (1847–1922) in due course provided much employment for female operators.

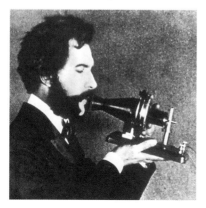

London calling: Alexander Graham Bell speaking into the

Centennial telephone, c. 1876: a truly epoch-making invention.

1865 The 1,700-ton St. Louis-to-New Orleans side-wheeler steamboat *Sultana* explodes on the Mississippi, killing over half of the 2,300 people on board.

1873 After 937 voyages, piracy and native hostility end the American pepper trade with Sumatra.

1893 Paris students witness the world's first striptease at the Bal des Quatre Arts: the artist's model who disrobes for the art students is fined 100 francs in court.

EVERY HOME SHOULD HAVE ONE

QWERTY

On early mechanical typewriters, the keys jammed when used at speed. Sholes arranged the keys so the most frequently used letters were separated, and the "qwerty" keyboard was born. Even today, the qwerty keyboard remains as a reminder of the word processor's origins.

Unlike the typewriter, the telephone had an obvious function. The industrialized countries were already "wired up" following the invention of the telegraph principle by *William COOKE* (1806–79) and *Charles WHEATSTONE* (1802–75) in Britain (1837) and *Joseph HENRY* (1797–1878) and *Samuel MORSE* (1791–1872) in the U.S. (1838). By 1850 there were 4,000 miles of lines in Britain. The telegraph's usefulness in transmitting important information led to its rapid expansion, so when the telephone was perfected, the infrastructure was already there. From its wood and brass origins, the telephone would eventually become a necessity for the masses rather than a luxury for the few.

WHAT SHOULD A TELEPHONE LOOK LIKE?

The very earliest telephones could be confused with cameras, because the materials and shape were very similar. Soon the "candlestick" type evolved, at a time when the human operator played a vital role in connecting callers. The first telephone with a dial operated by the user was patented in 1891

The American candlestick-style Epsom telephone, 1912.

by Almon Stowger, an undertaker, who was convinced that the girls at the exchange were giving his competitors news about the recently deceased. The dial system prevailed until push buttons in the 1970s.

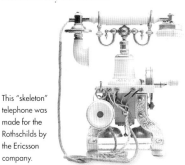

This "skeleton" telephone was made for the Rothschilds by the Ericsson company.

DESIGNER NAMES

With a scant knowledge of physics, **Marchese Gugliemo Marconi** *(1874–1937) became obsessed with the idea of wireless communication. Building on the experiments of Hertz, he sent a signal over a distance of one mile in 1895 and was transmitting across the Alantic by 1901. He lived to see radio become a home entertainment and a universal means of communication.*

1868 Rama V comes to the throne in Thailand; he will abolish slavery, introduce a postal and telegraph system, and open the country's first railroad.

1863 A scarlet fever epidemic in England takes more than 30,000 lives.

1875 A machine is invented to strip the kernels from corn cobs, and leads to wide-scale canning of corn.

1860~1900

Arty and Very Crafty
William Morris

William MORRIS (1834–96): a name in lights. Not just a hugely important British design captain, but one belonging to history, too. Morris was London-born to wealthy parents, and Oxford-educated; a craftsman in his own right, a major influence on European design, director of his own company, and a social reformer in the bargain.

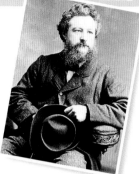

The Chairman: William Morris in 1877.

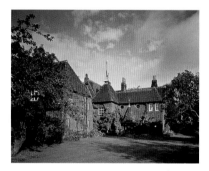

Architectural training under *G. E. STREET* (1824–81) left him with an incurable case of Victorian Gothic, but mercifully Morris was a lousy architect (and a worse painter) and opted to design himself into posterity. He wouldn't have made it without help from many gifted friends and contemporaries. Morris's closest chums were the architect *Philip WEBB* (1831–1915), and the Pre-Raphaelite painters *Ford MADOX BROWN* (1821–93), *Edward*

The Red House at Bexley Heath, Morris's dream house.

BURNE-JONES (1833–98), and *Dante Gabriel ROSSETTI* (1828–82). This unlikely bunch helped Morris build his home, "The Red House," at Bexley Heath, Kent, which he wanted to be "a small palace of art."

Morris was just as important as the founder of the nineteenth-century mega-design partnership of Morris, Marshall, Faulkner & Co (a.k.a. The Firm). The members parted company after a decade, but Morris kept the company name, and it outlasted him before folding in 1939.

A complex, intense, and humorless man, Morris was a pattern-maker at heart, and a perfectionist. Taking inspiration from the English countryside, Morris

The Thoughts of Chairman Morris…
…are best enshrined in his own book *News from Nowhere* (1890). Strange title? Some people think that Morris saw that he just wasn't getting through.

1876 American Henry A. Sherwin develops a machine that finely grinds pigments and suspends them in linseed oil to produce the first ready-to-apply paint.

1891 British butchers are accused of selling meat unfit for human consumption.

1900 Austrian pathologist Dr. Karl Landsteiner discovers the three different types of blood (he calls them Types A, B, and C).

began creating the patterns that made him famous during the 1880s. Loaded with meaning and devoid of abstraction, his designs related to real, natural themes. Ideal objects? Natural forms, of course, derived from plants and flowers, leaves, and fruits, with names like Artichoke, Lodden, and Evenlode. Design classics, every one, and still much imitated. Not even the all-enveloping white purity of the Modern movement could eclipse this stuff, and every mall and shopping street still stocks it somewhere.

The Kelmscott Press

Morris's indulgence was his Kelmscott Press, set up in 1890 to produce deluxe limited editions for the connoisseur. It's hard to match this activity with Morris's socialism, but that's the way it was. Even if Morris was pandering to the idle rich (his work didn't come cheap), Kelmscott gave him the chance to develop new ideas (or revive old ones) in typography.

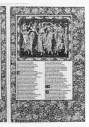

A characteristically ornate spread from the Kelmscott Press *Chaucer*, 1896.

EVERY HOME SHOULD HAVE ONE

Morris textiles

Actually every home should have as little as possible to do with Morris reproduction furnishing fabrics or wallpaper. In terms of real design, you need to think twice before you purchase. But if you must have it, go for the real thing. It's expensive but it's still being made, and you'll see the difference immediately. As with so many things, it's an acquired taste, and one I'm afraid I shan't be acquiring.

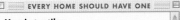

MAKING IT FOR EVERYMAN

Unlike some designers of his day, Morris wasn't trying to re-establish a medieval vernacular style. His agenda was to do with the relationships between the designer, the artifact itself, and the poor old worker churning out ghastly ornaments without a second thought. Where was the fun in that, eh? Morris loathed mass-production, but he understood its place in society. Most people agree that his ideas were basically Marxist. He wanted designers to understand their chosen materials; he wanted products to be made well, and with an understanding of the marketplace. He wanted quality. But hey, you can't have it all.

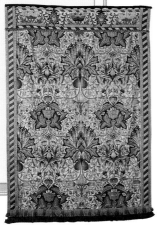

One of Morris's famous wall-hanging designs, Artichoke.

1863 Midget circus performer General Tom Thumb marries Lavinia Warren (a.k.a. Mercy Bunn), who is 2 feet 8 inches tall; the wedding attracts enormous crowds

1866 English physician Thomas Clifford Allbut invents the clinical thermometer.

1871 Following a request from Queen Victoria at a royal party, American ambassador Robert Cumming Schenck introduces her to the game of poker.

1870~1920

And So Say All of Us
The Arts and Crafts movement

A devotee of
Arts and Crafts

The Arts and Crafts movement wasn't exactly a design historical "ism," but it comes close. In real terms it was made up of several committed Morris supporters spreading the gospel of common aims and regional variations in design, and joy in labor (hallelujah). Yes, guys 'n' gals, you, too, can enjoy folksy, vernacular buildings and authentic Olde Englishe furnishings. Ye half-timbered houses and ye olde bearded men in smocks.

Some of the most fervent Morrisites even headed for the country with their converts, in an attempt to discover design purity. No wonder Morris disavowed them. *And* those tediously middle-aged guilds.

So, under "Arts and Crafts," please file the following: the Century Guild (1882) and its founder, A. H. MACKMURDO (1851–1942), who deserves a name-check for his chairs; the Art Worker's Guild (1884); and a big hand, please, for C. R. ASHBEE (1863–1942), whose Guild of Handicraft (1888) achieved enormous success with its silverware and jewelry in London's East End, and ended its days in the Oxfordshire countryside in 1908, where the locals were as friendly as Monet's were at Giverny. Not.

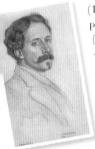

Charles Robert Ashbee, drawn in 1903 by William Strang.

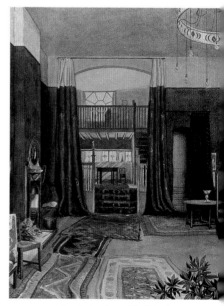

As typical an Arts and Crafts interior as you could wish to see, designed by Ashbee.

EVERY HOME SHOULD HAVE ONE

Something by Dresser

Anything at all: it's definitive stuff, even if it's extremely expensive. A serious collector will want to fill this important place in his/her pantheon. Metalwork is the most immediately accessible, but the glass is perfectly fine also. Go for it.

DRESSER SENSE

Christopher Dresser (1834–1904) was a South Kensington Schools success story and more: a Doctor of Botany and a veritable walking, talking, thinking-man's design prophet, whose brain left Chairman Morris's hemispheres looking withered. He saw the writing on the wall, calmly ignored the medieval posturings of the Arts and Crafts movement, and kept on trading—literally and metaphorically—on the belief that a good piece of design should combine function, simplicity, and mechanical skill.

If anyone took design and interior decoration into the realms of art, it was Dresser. His message to Morris was clear: quit whining and just accept the inevitability of industrial progress. Meet it halfway, with well-designed objects. To show he meant it, Dresser designed glass that beat Gallé and Tiffany hands down, conceived

A minimalist Dresser teapot in silver with a wooden handle, from 1881.

Handicrafts across the ocean

Arts and Crafts might have begun in Britain, but it went platinum in the U.S., in every category, not least Architectural Regionalism (not the 1930s painting style). Look at the American medieval-style architecture in St. Thomas's Church, New York (1905–20), and fabulous American versions of "vernacular" from Rhode Island to Pasadena.

St. Thomas's Church in Union Square, New York: Arts and Crafts' American Adventure.

metalwork that matched anything to be made in Europe years later, and still had time to become a market leader in Japanese ornament and architecture during the 1890s. Head and shoulders above his peers in the design game, Dresser made combinations of "fantasy and invention" that were hailed loudly by his contemporaries, and Art Nouveau would forever be in his debt.

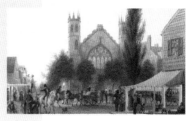

1862 The first Monte Carlo gambling casino opens in Monaco under the direction of the former casino manager at Bad Hamburg.

1866 William Morris, English craftsman, poet, and designer, introduces the Morris chair, designed to recline or fold up completely for travel.

1896 Radioactivity is discovered by French phycisist Antoine Henri Becquerel.

1860~1920

From Gears to Gas

On the road, one way or another

A genteel parade—but in practice they demanded some hard pedaling.

Safety bike? You must be joking. Joseph Starley's 1885 design for the "Rover Safety" bike seems misnamed by today's standards: it had no brakes. Well, you could back-pedal. At least if you stopped pedaling, you didn't tumble from a great height, as you did on the pennyfarthing style of bike. Its diamond frame and equal-size wheels seem sensible now, but they had taken some time to evolve. Soon all bikes looked like this, and the pennyfarthing fell out of favor.

The bicycle was one of the first products to be widely advertised, and was *the* desirable object of the 1880s. The world was on the move, and the bike had a

An upturned bathtub on wheels (or a 40hp Mercedes from 1902).

startling effect on peoples' lives, especially women. It wasn't just a means of getting around, but a focus of sporting and social activity. Freedom of mobility, which had been the privilege of those who could afford a horse, and a carriage to go with it, was now a possibility for the masses.

TWO WHEELS GOOD—
FOUR WHEELS BETTER

In Europe in the 1860s, various experimenters had been trying to design engines that ran on fuels other than coal. The earliest of these, like the machines of Frenchman *Etienne Lenoir* (1822–1900), ran on gas, and later benzene.

46

1909 Double-decker buses appear for the first time in the City of London.

1913 Coco Chanel pioneers sportswear for women at a new boutique in Deauville, featuring berets and open-necked shirts in an age when women of fashion wear feathers and huge hats.

1920 Meccano launches the Hornby Locomotive No. 1, the first of its stylish toy trains.

So what on earth do we do with this stuff?

Difficult as it might be to believe, gasoline, that essential commodity, which now moves a billion vehicles around, used to be a waste product. Bearded men drilling for water in Texas in the 1850s found this black oily goo by mistake, and discovered that some of it could be distilled for use in lamps to replace smelly fish oil. This fuel was known as paraffin in Britain, kerosene in the U.S. The distillers were left with a highly combustible liquid—petrol or gasoline—which had no obvious use, although it was sold as a patent cold cure just to try to get rid of it.

Nikolaus OTTO (1832–91), a penniless German inventor, improved on these new "internal combustion" engines when, in 1877, he patented a four-stroke engine that also ran on gas.

These were standing engines for powering pumps and machinery, and by 1900 there were 200,000 in use throughout Europe. In the 1890s the young German engineer *Gottlieb* DAIMLER (1834–1900) designed a lightweight engine to propel road vehicles, and his colleague *Wilhelm* MAYBACH (1846–1929) designed the first efficient carburetor that would make gasoline a feasible fuel—and thus the horseless carriage was born!

This wonder of the age was greeted with delight as a non-polluting machine—nothing more than a puff of exhaust came out. Horses were much more problematic, leaving piles of manure all over the streets. While the internal combustion engine was being developed, the bicycle industry had

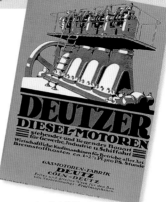

Poster promoting Rudolf Diesel's revolutionary engine, which ran on cheaper, less flammable fuel.

matured and grown. But now established cycle makers such as Hillman in England and Opel in Germany turned to the car, while in Detroit, a young man named Ford was having some ideas of his own...

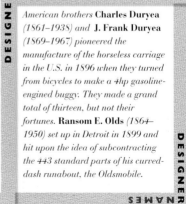

DESIGNER NAMES

American brothers **Charles Duryea** *(1861–1938) and* **J. Frank Duryea** *(1869–1967) pioneered the manufacture of the horseless carriage in the U.S. in 1896 when they turned from bicycles to make a 4hp gasoline-engined buggy. They made a grand total of thirteen, but not their fortunes.* **Ransom E. Olds** *(1864–1950) set up in Detroit in 1899 and hit upon the idea of subcontracting the 443 standard parts of his curved-dash runabout, the Oldsmobile.*

1894 In Washington, Senator Bradley forbids the projection of Edison's film *The Serpentine Dance* in which dancer Carmencita shows her underwear, creating the first case of censorship in the film industry.

1900 Coca-Cola is launched in Britain, 14 years after it was first drunk in the U.S.

1901 In New York City actors at the Academy of Music are arrested for wearing costumes on a Sunday.

1880~1940

Say Cheese
Cameras

Can you imagine going on vacation without a camera? We take it for granted, but as a common object it has been around for only about 120 years. American George EASTMAN (1854–1932) did more than invent a practical cheap camera, he also invented a catchy trade name: Kodak. This was no acronym, or his name backward or some such trick. He deliberately devised a word that he thought would be memorable, and clearly succeeded.

George Eastman, 1930, creator of snapshot photography.

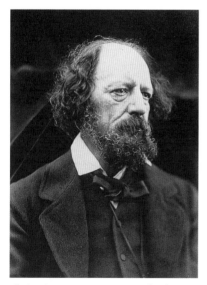

The key to his success was the arrival of clear celluloid film that could be treated with chemicals to make a compact roll. Previously photographers had to lug heavy glass plates around and process these themselves. With Eastman's process, much like the "throwaway" cameras of today, you sent the whole camera back to the factory for processing. One roll produced 100 pictures.

Alfred, Lord Tennyson, Victorian England's Poet Laureate, giving a photo opportunity for Julia Margaret Cameron to show her camera skills.

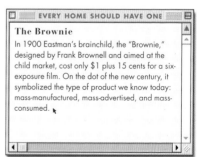

EVERY HOME SHOULD HAVE ONE

The Brownie

In 1900 Eastman's brainchild, the "Brownie," designed by Frank Brownell and aimed at the child market, cost only $1 plus 15 cents for a six-exposure film. On the dot of the new century, it symbolized the type of product we know today: mass-manufactured, mass-advertised, and mass-consumed.

1904 American businessman Thomas Sullivan invents the tea bag.

1912 The first self-service food store opens, in California.

1930 A *London Graphic* writer coins the phrase "candid camera" to describe the irreverent and intimate Leica portraits of statesmen made by German photographer Erich Solomon.

It was not just the economics of the camera that made it so attractive—it was its portability. In 1888 a whole new type of photography came about: the snapshot. Cameras no longer had to be on tripods, and a new informal style of photograph emerged. The family photo album changed from a collection of stilted studio portraits to something more lively. Eastman's genius provided the possibility of relatively cheap, simple photography.

A Kodak No. 3 camera from 1901: photography comes to the masses.

Photography was a suitable pursuit for ladies, one of whom, *Julia Margaret Cameron* (1815–79), became well known as a portraitist. She converted her coal hole into a darkroom, and her direct photographic portraiture was received with great acclaim.

The camera typifies many of the modern machines that we have around us. It does not perform an essential function, but it does make life more interesting and exciting.

LIFE IN THE CAMERA AGE

Kodak had many imitators, and soon black-and-white photography became commonplace. By the late 1890s advances in printing techniques allowed photographs to replace the somber, often intricately executed wood engravings that had illustrated books and magazines in the nineteenth century.

"Popular–Pleasant–Profitable" read the slogan above this advertisement: a winning combination then as now.

1874 French "Impressionists" hold their first exhibition at Paris in an independent show of paintings, including Claude Monet's *Impression: Sunrise.*

1874 The ice cream soda is invented when Robert Green runs out of cream for his syrup, sweet cream, and carbonated water mixture and substitutes vanilla ice cream.

1897 London's Moss Bros. of Covent Garden goes into the suit rental business at the request of an out-of-work stockbroker who has been given a job as a monologuist.

1870~1925

Music and Voices—Captured!
Sound recording

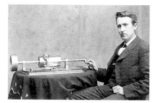

Super-inventor Thomas Edison and his phonograph.

What we take for granted today—recorded sound—was once regarded as magic, or possibly even witchcraft. In an age of wonder inventions like the typewriter, sewing machine, bicycle, and camera, wouldn't it be wonderful to be able to record the human voice?

Edison's Standard Model A, a big seller in the Jazz Age phonograph market.

Various inventors were trying to crack the problem in the 1870s; the prolific, workaholic *Thomas EDISON* (1847–1931) devised and patented a working model of his hand-cranked tinfoil cylinder design in 1877. He didn't foresee the potential of a music industry, but imagined the public would install machines in graveyards to hear the voices of lost loved ones. The first home machine sold in 1878 for $10, but the quality of the sound was so poor that it didn't catch on.

Ten years later, following the introduction of the improved wax cylinder, German immigrant *Emile*

BERLINER (1851–1929) patented the flat disk that was to set the pattern for sound recording for a hundred years. This made prerecorded music much easier to manufacture and market. Up to then, the only sort of music you could buy was sheet music—or of course an instrument that you had to learn to play. Now, like the camera, which had made everyone an artist, the gramophone (a term coined in 1888) made everyone a musician. We still talk about "playing" a record.

1907 Radio pioneer Lee De Forest invents electrical high-frequency "radio" surgery.

1915 Kafka's *Metamorphosis* is published, featuring a giant insect.

1920 Australian opera singer Nellie Melba makes recording history by becoming the first professional singer to be paid to perform on radio, with her rendition of Puccini's "Home Sweet Home."

Old faithful

Early records had their titles engraved on the center, but in 1900 the first paper label was designed by the Consolidated Talking Machine Company. This became one of the best-known trademarks of the recording industry: HMV—His Master's Voice. It reproduced a touching painting by Francis Barraud of a dog called Nipper listening to his dead master's voice.

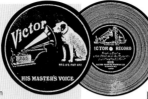

His Master's Voice: the touching image of an attentive Nipper.

The first electric sound recordings were made in the early 1920s, and this became a commercial process in 1925 on both sides of the Atlantic. In the same year, the first all-electric phonograph with amplified sound, the Brunswick Panotrope, was launched in Iowa, complete with a volume control. Up to then, when you wanted less sound, you uttered the immortal phrase "put a sock in it."

WIND ME UP

The new wonder machine caught the public imagination. The simple mechanical wind-up gramophone, playing disks at 78 r.p.m. (one of the first internationally agreed standards), transformed home entertainment. The material that the new disks were made from—shellac—was the forerunner of today's mass-produced plastic products, albeit a natural one. Obtained from the secretions of the lac beetle, shellac was used to make records until the 1950s, when it was replaced by vinyl.

Incredibly, as early as 1903, the opera star Enrico Caruso had made a million-selling recording of "Vesti la giubba" from *I Pagliacci*. By World War I, the gramophone had become portable, and raised morale in the trenches with some of the earliest jazz tunes like "The Livery Stable Blues." When the war was over, the gramophone became the stylish addition to the 1920s picnic and the flapper's cocktail party, and the latest records would be available in their brown paper sleeves in your local music store.

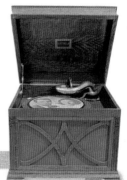

The flat-disk gramophone superseded the cylinder phonograph in the 1880s.

1893 The first Ferris Wheel goes up at the World's Columbian Exposition in Chicago: 250 feet in diameter, it has 36 forty-seat passenger cars at its rim.

1897 French cinematographer Georges Méliès dares to introduce on-screen nudity for the first time, in his film entitled *After the Ball*.

1898 German chemical-pharmaceutical firm Farbenfabriken vorm. Friedrich Bayer und Co. introduces heroin as a cough suppressant.

1890~1910

Curly Wurly, Airy-Fairy

Art Nouveau

A title page by Fritz Erler for the weekly journal *Jugend*, August 1896.

Here's the myth: the Naughty Nineties begin, and just as Arts and Crafts's straight lines and nasty angles are beginning to pall, Art Nouveau descends over Europe in a decadent pink cloud and excites everyone from Glasgow to Vienna with its new, easy-flowing lines, bobsled curves, loop-the-loop spirals, and rich ornamentation.

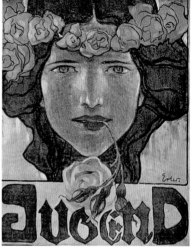

Not so simple. Sure, Art Nouveau was as new as its name and its new shapes, but its roots were entangled in the natural forms of Arts and Crafts, and age-old concerns about form, function, ornament, and structure bedeviled the new style. The name itself came from Paris, where *Samuel BING* (1838–1905) gave his Japanese art store a makeover in 1895. He called it La Maison de l'Art Nouveau, began to show, sell, and commission one-off work by contemporary European artists, and, presto, a sensation. It caught on, lasted a few years, and was over well before 1914.

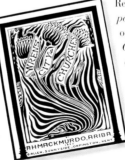

Art Nouveau emerges? The title page of *Wren's City Churches* (1883).

PLANT LIFE REVISITED

Remember A. H. Mackmurdo *(see page 44)*? The flowing plant forms on the title page of his book *Wren's City Churches* (1883) were developed from William Morris *(see page 42)*, but they're often given as the first manifestation of Art Nouveau. New graphics, new designs, in new 1890s magazines like *The Studio*, *Jugend*, *Pan*, and *Ver Sacrum* sent Art Nouveau's creepers throughout the northern hemisphere.

1901 The Metropolitan Police in London installs the first fingerprint file at its headquarters, Scotland Yard, as a means of tracing and identifying criminals.

1903 Britain sets up the National Art Collections Fund to prevent works of art from leaving the country.

1906 German-born hairdresser Karl Nessler launches the "permanent wave" in a London salon: the whole process takes 8 to 12 hours.

A Tiffany glass lampshade: Art Nouveau icon, and model for countless plastic imitations.

Everyone has a mental picture of Art Nouveau, but even its contemporaries found it hard to be exact. Some Italians called it *Stile Liberty* (after the London store), and the Germans called their version *Jugendstil* (literally, "youth-style"). In truth, Art Nouveau was diverse and derivative, looking backward and forward, sometimes both at once. It was a melting pot that could cope with studio glass by *Émile Gallé* (1846–1904) and *Louis Comfort Tiffany* (1848–1933); the Franco-Belgian architecture of Baron *Victor Horta* (1861–1947); the furniture of *C. R. Mackintosh* (1868–1928); and much more.

EVERY HOME SHOULD HAVE ONE

Mucha posters

You don't need that Tiffany or Gallé glass! What you really want is an original poster by Alphonse Mucha. Not just any poster: it has to be one of his classic Sarah Bernhardts. He made more than a few, so you can take your pick, though finding one for yourself is a little difficult.

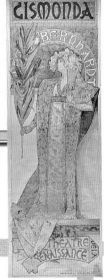

An enduring image of Art Nouveau: Mucha's *Gismonda*. More such posters followed, especially of Sarah Bernhardt.

DESIGNER NAMES

Moravian-born **Alphonse Mucha** *(1860–1939) was the graphic designer whose poster* Gismonda *(1894) transformed the career of actress Sarah Bernhardt. Mucha's period pin-ups on posters, menus, calendars, and in his style-books secured him a lasting reputation throughout Europe. When boredom set in, Mucha tried to reinvent himself in the U.S. (1904–09), only to find that Americans wanted him in his European incarnation, not as some newly reconstituted portrait painter. He headed back to Austria-Hungary to paint his vast, mind-blowing series of canvases,* The Slav Epic.

The States were also unkind to **Archibald Knox** *(1864–1933). His Celtic-inspired, biomorphic studio metalwork and textiles were huge hits at the London emporium of* **Sir Arthur Liberty** *(1843–1917). Then taste changed, Liberty dumped him, and Knox set off for the U.S. in 1912. A year was enough, and by 1913 he was back in the Isle of Man, drifting into obscurity.*

DESIGNER NAMES

1851 German entrepreneur Paul Julius Reuter founds the Reuters News Service, following his previous success using carrier pigeons to convey messages.

1893 Chicago surgeon Daniel Hale Williams performs the world's first open-heart surgery, saving the life of a street fighter with a knife wound in an artery near his heart.

1896 London's National Portrait Gallery (Tate Gallery) moves from Bethnal Green to its new home in Westminster and is completed with money donated by sugar magnate Sir Henry Tate.

1850~1918

Print It, Paste It
Posters

The poster of the mid-nineteenth century was a pretty plain affair, dominated by typography. However, it did stimulate some novel type designs, breaking the rules about how letters should be constructed. Out went the classic Roman principles, and in came sans serif: plain letters using even-thickness lines, with no twiddly bits at the ends of each line. Other innovations were condensed lettering (horizontally squashed) and extended lettering (horizontally stretched).

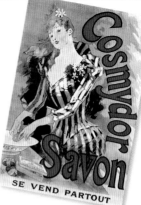

Jules Cheret served advertisers well, capturing the color and swirl of Paris.

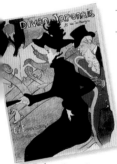

Toulouse-Lautrec's poster for that delightful play, *Divan Japonais.*

Posters told people what was going on—and, with the coming of mass production, what to buy. In an age before radio and TV, posters and press ads were the only ways to sell.

New technology—large-scale color lithography—transformed the poster from the 1860s on, allowing it to break away from the stranglehold of type and become illustrated. The pioneer of the pretty poster was *Jules CHERET* (1836–1932), who designed more than 2,000 posters between 1860 and 1900 and inspired *Pierre BONNARD* (1867–1947) and *Henri de TOULOUSE-LAUTREC* (1864–1901) to cross the divide between fine art and design. The exotic bustle of Montmartre and *fin-de-siècle* night life were captured in Cheret's swirling colors. The billboard became the poor man's art gallery.

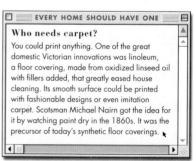

EVERY HOME SHOULD HAVE ONE

Who needs carpet?

You could print anything. One of the great domestic Victorian innovations was linoleum, a floor covering, made from oxidized linseed oil with fillers added, that greatly eased house cleaning. Its smooth surface could be printed with fashionable designs or even imitation carpet. Scotsman Michael Nairn got the idea for it by watching paint dry in the 1860s. It was the precursor of today's synthetic floor coverings.

1901 In Berlin Eugene Hollander performs the world's first facelift, on a Polish aristocrat who has supplied her own drawings for the occasion.

1909 A futurist manifesto by Italian poet-publicist Emilio Filippo Tommaso Marinetti advocates rejecting the past, including use of syntax and grammatical rules.

1912 The New York Journal is the first newspaper to include a crossword puzzle.

Two British painters, *James PRIDE* (1866–1949) and *William NICHOLSON* (1872–1949), decided to turn their hand to poster design to earn some cash. As "the Beggerstaff Brothers," they produced some startlingly simple—i.e., modern—designs. Simplicity also marked German poster design of the 1900s from master designers like *Lucian BERNHARD* (1883–1972), *Hans ERDT* (1838–1918), and *Ludwig HOHLWEIN* (1874–1949). Their images, reduced to the bare minimum in flat, strong colors and bold headlines, shrugged off Art Nouveau twiddles.

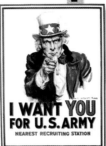

I WANT YOU
FOR U.S. ARMY
NEAREST RECRUITING STATION

1917 U.S. Army recruitment poster.

DESIGNER NAMES

By 1914, poster advertising was a fine art, and ministries of propaganda across the globe used great graphic designers to influence civilian hearts and minds at home and abroad. Help! Save! Support! Enlist! were just some of the photo-lithographic cries that shrilled from billboards. British servicemen grew to hate an **Alfred Leete** *(1882–1933) recruiting poster bearing the image of Lord Kitchener (1914); the American equivalent featuring Uncle Sam (1917) was designed by* **James Montgomery Flagg** *(1877–1960).*

DESIGNER NAMES

THE HALFTONE REVOLUTION

The "halftone" was perfected in the 1890s, allowing photographs to be converted to small dots and printed on ordinary paper. This made photo-magazines and popular newspapers possible: the first was the London *Daily Mail*.

Color printing meant that illustrators like *Edmund DULAC* (1882–1953) and *Arthur RACKHAM* (1867–1939) could have their artwork faithfully reproduced. Stationery items such as greeting cards, valentines, and wrapping paper were also invented at this time.

Victorian Valentines were one (good?) use for color printing.

As bark on storm-tossed foam

In harbour safe would be, My heart no more to roam.

Would anchor, Love, with thee.

With Love

HEART'S DELIGHT

To my VALENTINE

1900 The trademark "His Master's Voice" label with a picture of Nipper, the fox terrier, listening to a gramophone, appears on records for the first time.

1906 The hot dog gets its name from a cartoon by Chicago cartoonist Thomas Aloysius "Tad" Dorgan showing a dachshund inside a frankfurter bun.

1910 French pharmacist Émile Coué suggests the slogan "Every day, in every way, I'm growing better and better," for auto-suggestive healing.

1900~1950

Which Way to Go?
New century, new ideas

Art Nouveau was one of the main end-of-century fads, but there were also other changes in the air, and for once there wasn't a war on. The whole spectrum of creative activity was in a state of ferment. Improved communication and contacts among artists, craftsmen, and designers led to a wide debate about the direction in which design should go.

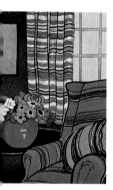

A design for modern cottage furniture from *Studio* magazine, c. 1920.

Although Morris's and Ruskin's principles had been an inspiration to mainland European theorists *(see page 42)*, the Europeans took design down a more rational route, and the blending of art and commerce became their goal. A lively debate emerged in Europe about the principles of design, encouraged by the internationally minded *Studio* magazine founded in England in 1893.

DESIGNER NAMES

Probably the first corporate designer was **Peter Behrens** *(1868–1940). Like other designers of this period, he started as an artist-craftsman, but gravitated toward industrial design, doing packaging and publicity for AEG from 1903. In 1907, he became AEG's architect and all-round design supremo, one of the first designers to have a corporate view. He designed AEG's factories, logos, and products. His 1908 electric copper kettle has a quaint Arts and Crafts look with its rattan cover handle, but the electric fan of the same year is a thoroughly modern product.*

These were products for the new age, made by modern mass-production methods. Behrens was an inspired designer in many fields—furniture, glass, ceramics, jewelry—and was the godfather of modern architecture, as Le Corbusier, Gropius, and Mies van der Rohe all worked in his practice. He was also instrumental in the establishment of the Deutscher Werkbund in 1907, which became a big influence in advancing good, modern design among German manufacturers.

A nickel-plated kettle designed by Behrens for AEG in 1908.

1914 The Panama Canal is opened to traffic on August 15.

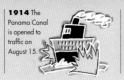

1931 Rio de Janeiro's Christ the Redeemer is dedicated on the city's Corcovado (Hunchback Mountain). The concrete statue is 125-feet tall, 92 feet across, and weighs 1,145 tons.

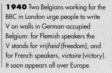

1940 Two Belgians working for the BBC in London urge people to write V on walls in German-occupied Belgium: for Flemish speakers the V stands for *vrijheid* (freedom), and for French speakers, *victoire* (victory). It soon appears all over Europe.

Happy on the soapbox was vociferous Belgian *Henry van de Velde* (1863–1957), architect, designer, craft factory owner, and writer. He was enthusiastic about Arts and Crafts principles, but was more prepared to accept factory production, insisting on the artist's creative input. He was a pioneer of the Deutscher Werkbund, established in 1907, a group of enlightened Germans from all walks of life who believed in the need for well-designed mass-produced goods. A fellow founder was *Richard Riemerschmidt* (1868–1957), another all-rounder whose 1907 furniture designs were dubbed "machine furniture."

NOTHING SUCCEEDS LIKE SECESSION

In prosperous Austria, radical young artists and designers had broken the yoke of tradition and founded the Vienna Secession in 1898 to put a line in the sand between them and what they regarded as old hat. *Koloman Moser* (1868–1918) was a brilliant graphic designer, and with architect *Josef Hoffmann* (1870–1956) founded the Wiener Werkstätte in

Filling the shelves

"You are what you own" became evident as more and more goods were mass-produced and more people could afford them. The historian Asa Briggs has even written a book called *Victorian Things*. For the most part, though, not a lot of thought went into how these things looked. The design of goods was largely guided by copying past styles and responding to the demand for products that aped the taste of the aristocracy. There was a widening gulf between the craft-made object and the advancing use of manufacturing techniques that cut out laborious handwork such as casting and pressing. The rise of manufacturing particularly distressed William Morris and his well-heeled friends, who could afford to have good taste *(see pages 42–43)*.

1903. In contrast to curvy Art Nouveau, Hoffmann fell in love with the right angle. An all-round (sorry, all-square) 3D designer, he produced some startlingly modern trays, flatware, and furniture.

Hoffmann was inspired by like-minded *Charles Rennie Mackintosh* (1868–1928), whom he visited in 1903. The stark simplicity and straight lines of Mackintosh's architecture and furniture was on the same wavelength, and the Austrians loved it. Zeitgeist? You bet.

Sit up straight with Charles Rennie Mackintosh, not a man for slouching.

1892 Iowa engineer Joseph Smith Duncan invents the Addressograph, a machine that prints mailing addresses automatically.

1901 Edison General Electric Co. introduces Christmas tree lights to the American public for the first time.

1907 In New York, the 47-story Singer Building is completed and becomes the world's tallest skyscraper.

1860~1940

Shocking Developments
Electricity

Joseph Swan, inventor of the lightbulb (ahead of Edison).

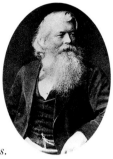

If the nineteenth century was the age of steam, the twentieth was the age of electricity. Among other new wonders, this made the electric chair a new, humane way of disposing of criminals. What had begun as scientific novelty in the early nineteenth century emerged as the new "clean" energy source of the twentieth. Coal and gas didn't disappear in a flash, so to speak, but were gradually replaced by this much more acceptable, mysterious stuff that came down wires.

Its first dramatic impact was in lighting. *Joseph Swan* (1828–1914) had invented the first working lightbulbs with carbon filaments in 1860, and when Edison caught up with him in the 1880s in a blaze of publicity, they settled their patent disputes out of court. Swan's house was the first in Britain to be lit

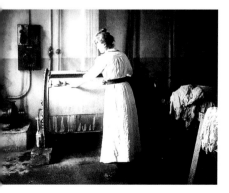

Electric washing machines (this one's from 1915) took some of the drudgery out of housework.

by electricity, shortly followed by the House of Commons in 1884. (Prior to the incandescent bulb, there had been public spaces lit by carbon arcs, but these were very harsh and needed constant adjustment.) The sheer convenience of electric lighting made it very popular and desirable. No more lamps to fill, or wicks or mantles to light, just the flick of a switch. Household servants had their lives transformed, but they had to be instructed not to throw water over sparking switches.

The more powerful electric current needed for both heating and cooking did not become available until the power stations were upgraded to provide electricity for city trams. The electricity companies encouraged its use for cooking and heating, and a

1908 Buick Motor Car president W. C. Durant and French-American motorcycle specialist Albert Champion found the AC Spark Plug Co.

1932 More than 10 million Americans are unemployed as a result of the Great Depression.

1936 Tokyo geisha Sada Abeis is arrested for stabbing her unfaithful lover Kichizo Ishida to death in his sleep, castrating him, and carrying his penis about in her sash for three days while eluding police.

Everybody's favorite. What did children eat before the 1930s?

Freeze it
Pioneer food preserver Clarence Birdseye (yes, his real name) had been perfecting the freezing of food since 1915. He made his fortune selling his process, and his name, for $22 million in 1929, just before the Wall Street crash.

bitter advertising war between gas and electricity companies broke out. The Electricity Board of London scored a goal with the slogan "Don't kill your wife with work—let electricity do it!," for although gas was explosive and poisonous, electric shocks were a new hazard.

Primitive versions of many types of electrical gadgets had been designed by 1900, but they were manufactured in very small quantities, since only the wealthy had ready access to electricity. Early electrical appliances were also notoriously unreliable, but as technology improved and electrical supplies spread, more households could enjoy the luxury of labor-saving devices. The servant shortage following World War I made these gadgets all the more desirable.

A middle-class family paying reverential attention to a new arrival.

EVERY HOME SHOULD HAVE ONE

Oh, so cool

Probably the most significant innovation was the refrigerator. Keeping things cool had depended on a supply of ice. In the eighteenth century, the landed gentry solved this problem by chopping up their frozen lakes in winter and putting them in ice houses to chill their white wine and make that most exotic dessert, ice cream. When industrial refrigeration became possible in the 1850s, you could have ice delivered to keep in an insulated wooden cabinet, the precursor of the refrigerator as we know it. The first electric home refrigerator, the Domelre from Chicago, appeared in 1913, and by the 1920s a well-known brand was on the market, the Frigidaire.

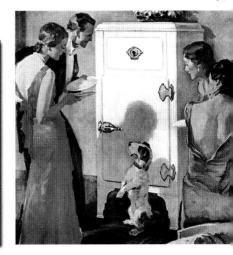

1885 General Gordon is killed in Khartoum in Mahdi's Muslim "holy war."

1918 Louis Cartier, brother of Paris jeweler Pierre and designer of the first wristwatch, introduces the Tank watch in tribute to the men of the American Tank Corps.

1919 Commander of the German fleet Rear-Admiral von Reuter commands his seamen to scuttle their own ships at Scapa Flow, Orkney Islands, to avoid handing them over to the Allies.

1860~1945
Designing for Doom
Weaponry

It's a paradox. Warfare brings out the beast in humans, but the best in design. Three centuries separate Leonardo's flying machine and armored-car concepts from modern battle tanks and B52s, but since the 1850s we've managed to perfect some extraordinary weaponry—and also the means of convincing ourselves that it's okay to use it.

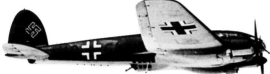

Cavalry of the air: the Luftwaffe goes into action in its Heinkel He IIIs.

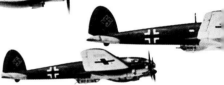

If *Richard GATLING* (1818–1903) hadn't patented his sophisticated hand-cranked machine gun in 1862, someone else would have matched him. Gatling's weapon managed 700 rounds per minute, and by 1884 *Hiram MAXIM* (1840–1916) perfected the automatic weapon that—with national variations—dominated every battlefield until 1945.

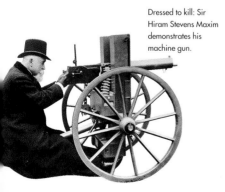

Dressed to kill: Sir Hiram Stevens Maxim demonstrates his machine gun.

The skies soon came into the equation. Being air-minded seemed increasingly natural after the Wright Brothers flew at Kitty Hawk (1903), and Louis Blériot's leap across the English Channel in a monoplane (1909) silenced military pooh-poohers at a stroke. Think of the possibilities! From then until 1919, designers wrestled with aerodynamic shapes, first as flying observation platforms and then as fighting machines. Sopwith, Fokker, Gotha, Nieuport, Boeing, Douglas, Avro, Hawker, Supermarine, Junkers, Heinkel, and Messerschmitt. Names to kill with, and brilliant designers, too. Not to mention that old windbag, Count Zeppelin.

1928 In Italy, Mussolini pronounces handshaking to be unhygienic.

1931 Cigarette advertisements claim that smoking is not only stylish, but also good for you.

1943 Americans are told to "use it up, wear it out, make it do, or do without."

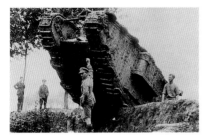

Britain's secret weapon seems to have got a bit stuck in the mud.

Amazingly. it happened. The new vehicle was called "Tank" to deceive the enemy, and evolved in a fever of intense activity in Britain during 1915–16. In September 1916 the first went into action in France. It jolted, unsprung, across no-man's land at 3.7 MPH. It was a start.

RULING THE WAVES, OR TRYING TO

In 1904 Britain's Royal Navy designed and launched its first Dreadnought battleship: faster, better armored, and better gunned than anything then afloat. Everyone was envious, especially the German Kaiser, so Britain and Germany had a battleship race.

This situation exercised other minds on both sides. Why attack a battleship head on, if instead you can use…a submarine? Submersibles had been around since the 1620s (yes!), and Americans, French, and British took the ideas further. In 1914 the Germans showed their enemies how to use this new weapon, by sinking three British cruisers in one hour. The rest is history.

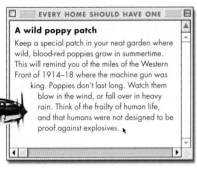

EVERY HOME SHOULD HAVE ONE

A wild poppy patch

Keep a special patch in your neat garden where wild, blood-red poppies grow in summertime. This will remind you of the miles of the Western Front of 1914–18 where the machine gun was king. Poppies don't last long. Watch them blow in the wind, or fall over in heavy rain. Think of the frailty of human life, and that humans were not designed to be proof against explosives.

MAKING TRACKS

Most people credit Leonardo da Vinci with the concept of the tank, but until 1915 no two people could agree to design and build one. Necessity provided the spur when World War I turned into entrenched deadlock. Artillery and the machine gun governed every front. Generals needed to reintroduce movement to a situation where cavalry were redundant. The brief: design and build a machine to break the enemy's line, capable of fighting across badly broken ground and proof against machine-gun ammunition.

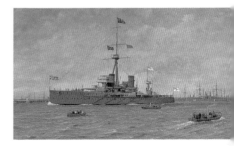

Dreadnought Class battleships changed the face of sea warfare.

1900 In New York Heinz erects an electric sign six stories high with 1,200 lights listing "57 Good Things for the Table"; these include Heinz tomato soup, tomato ketchup, sweet pickles, India relish, and peach butter.

1914 The relief ship SS *Massapequa* arrives in Belgium carrying a cargo of food sent by the Rockefeller Foundation to aid the starving Belgians.

1921 Gandhi announces that he is rejecting Western clothing and will henceforth wear only a loincloth and shawl.

1900~1935

Primary Objectives
De Stijl

The style. Such authority! De Stijl was first formed in 1917 as a magazine, the mouthpiece of a group of like-minded and creative Dutchmen, who then gave themselves the same name. Led by architect and painter Theo van DOESBURG (1883–1931) and including architect J. J. P. OUD (1890–1963) and the painter Piet MONDRIAN (1872–1944), they were an odd bunch. Their aims? Calvinist simplicity, spirituality through abstraction, and the unity of the arts and society.

Are you sitting stylishly? Gerrit Rietveld's Zig Zag chair.

Love and peace? Who could blame them after World War I? De Stijl thought intense thoughts, used primary colors (red, yellow, and blue) for painted surfaces, divided the color areas with the straightest black lines in Europe, and called this process "Neo-plasticism."

Incredibly, it was a hit. De Stijl's austere ideas caught on, and Mondrian became a cult figure. But in the field of design, the most influential Stijlite was a slightly later joiner, *Gerrit Thomas RIETVELD* (1888–1964). Young Gerrit was self-taught, a doer, not

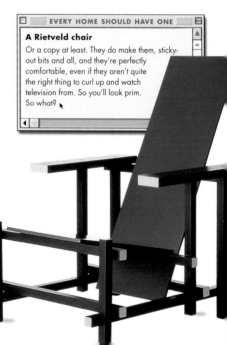

The Red/Blue chair was revolutionary in construction as well as appearance.

1931 Clairol hair dye is introduced by U.S. chemists' broker Lawrence Gelb, 33, who had acquired the formula in Europe.

1932 After nine years of work, the Zuider Zee (Ijsselmeer) is reclaimed, creating a new area of Dutch farmland.

1935 Charles Darrow invents the board game Monopoly. The object of the game is to bankrupt the other players.

Style star

Gerrit Rietveld made the so-called minor art of furniture into something amazing, far out, ahead of its time, and the equal of painting and architecture. He called his Red/Blue Chair "a piece of space brought to life as reality." Can one go farther?

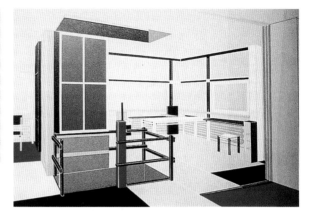

Esoteric play of line and space: the Schröder House in Utrecht.

a theorist. He'd always liked messing about with wood to see what happened, and his most famous object, the Red/Blue Chair (c.1918), was the result of some inspired messing. Hey! Hold those really nasty angles and bits that stick out...let's see what they do to this chair.

Contrary? It was cool. Keeping purity, spatial harmony, straight lines, and nasty angles firmly in focus, GR designed the Schröder House (1924) in Utrecht, a completely integrated color scheme inside and out, and a model of De Stijl design philosophy, with intersecting lines and planes and changing rectilinear spaces.

SPREADING AND FADING

With peace, international understanding, and spiritualism high on the human agenda, in the 1920s Theo van D went design walkabout and lectured at the Bauhaus in 1921 and in Paris in 1924;

in between he had met the revolutionary Russian Constructivist architect *El LISSITSKY* (1890–1941), and each had admired the other in print.

Although De Stijl preached unity, it was just about the most suspicious art/design group in Europe. It began to unravel when Mondrian left the group in 1925, and when Theo van D collaborated with Dadaists Hans and Sophie Arp in 1926, equilibrium went out the window. It was Theo's last collaboration, and the final issue of *De Stijl* carried his obituary. Sad.

The name endureth forever...

In 1999 a well-known maker of vacuum cleaners called one of its models—you guessed!—De Stijl, "in honor" of the Dutch design group. Naturally this object is molded in primary-colored plastic. And of course, one thinks high thoughts as one trundles through one's household chores.

1900 In China, the secret Society of Harmonious Fist believes members can use Taoist sorcery and magical incantations to make them impervious to bullets.

1905 Fifty British drivers band together to found the Automobile Association as a reaction against the growing hostility and antagonism toward cars.

1918 Emergency tent hospitals go up throughout the U.S. as the Spanish influenza epidemic exhausts regular hospital facilities.

1900~1935

Idealism, Pragmatism, Communism
Revolutionary Russia

There had been artistic ferment in Tsarist Russia long before the Revolution of 1917. Although it was on the outskirts of Europe, Russia had had close cultural ties with points West, particularly Paris, and the wild new ideas of cubism and abstraction had inspired the Russian avant-garde.

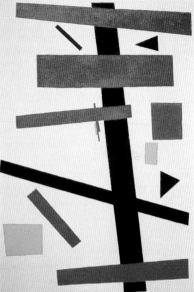

Abstract suprematism from Malevitch, juxtaposing brutally simple shapes and colors.

Creating a new Soviet state gave designers a golden opportunity to contribute to a new, better, fairer world. However, this led to a classic clash of art vs. functionalism, and a rash of ideas and concepts rarely got beyond the prototype stage.

Painter *Kasimir MALEVITCH* (1878–1935) pioneered a brand of simplified geometric visions to which he gave the term "suprematism." This could also be applied to architecture or to everyday objects. The artist-designer-engineer was looked upon as a savior who would create a comfortable, efficient modern world for the worker state.

Others thought that artists were a bunch of self-indulgent Bohemians, a hangover from the bad old days. What place did art have in this brave new world? The proletariat could design for their own needs, could they not? It would involve blending the ideals of communism, modernity, and technological efficiency.

Nice try...
In the heady revolutionary days when everything seemed possible, Vladimir Tatlin (1885–1953) set about designing and building the "Letatlin" air bicycle. It was to be a human-powered non-polluting machine based on birds' wings and glider principles. He dreamed of its being in everyday use, but as a precursor of the hang glider, it was a dismal failure.

1918 Russia adopts the Gregorian calendar—a solar dating system introduced by Pope Gregory XIII in 1582 and already in use throughout much of the Western world.

1921 Columbia University medical school graduate Armand Hammer goes to help the Lenin government cope with its postwar diseases and collect $150,000 owed to his father's company for drugs shipped during the Allied blockade of Russian ports.

1935 Stalin begins his campaign of show trials, purges, and deportations to forced labor camps with the help of his secret police.

CONSTRUCT-IT KIT

The new concept that emerged was Constructivism—a design principle that involved inspired use of mass-produced materials combined into new forms: Lego plus imagination plus social purpose. It could be applied to the graphics of *El Lissitsky* (1890–1941) or the furniture design of *Alexander Rodchenko* (1891–1956).

Unfortunately, little of this creativity had any effect on the lives of the workers of the new Soviet state, and the avant-garde soon fell into disfavor when Stalin rose to power. Their ideas did travel, however: De Stijl in Holland and the Bauhaus in Germany listened and—sometimes—acted.

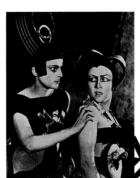

A scene from the film *Aelita*, showing Aleksandra Ekster's futuristic costume designs.

Textile design by Lyubov Popova for a lightweight fabric.

A cheery book advertisement from 1924 by Varvara Stepanova.

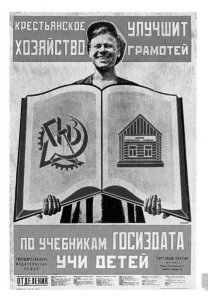

1926 Louis Armstrong records "scat singing"—improvised wordless sounds—in the song "Heebie Jeebies."

1929 Vatican City is established, the smallest independent country in the world.

1931 A scene from Charlie Chaplin's movie *City Lights*, in which a blind flower seller recognizes him as a rich man, takes a record 323 takes to get right.

1920~1940

New Angles

Art Deco

Sunburst chic.

What was it about Art Deco? This very long moment in design began at the 1925 Paris International Exhibition of Decorative and Industrial Arts (les Arts Décoratifs, vous savez?). The expo was heavily subsidized by the French government: Art Nouveau and national pride had been bosom pals, and the French wanted more of the same.

Exhibitors at the show were told to be as "modern" as possible, so most used the linear forms of contemporary abstract art in their exhibits, but the heavyweight French design teams went one better and used the same streamlined abstraction in their plans for pavilions representing the most famous department stores—Galeries Lafayette, Printemps, and so on—and it all went intergalactic. "Art Deco" was the term used to describe this style, and its success was such that it penetrated nearly every level of design, and most sections of society, to the early 1940s.

Au revoir, Art Nouveau! In came clean-cut lines and feminine curves to replace the swirling plant forms. Objects were decorated in ways that we'd probably call "ethnic" today, with strong echoes of Egypt and South America in their shapes. At its most opulent top end, Art Deco was well suited to the production of luxurious

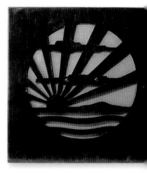

It's that sunburst again, here featured on a 1927 Pye wireless loudspeaker.

🖥️ **EVERY HOME SHOULD HAVE ONE**

The sunburst motif

This is a design classic; as a mid-century person, you'd see it everywhere. There'd be a sunburst on your front windows, and maybe your front gate, or your chair backs. The tiled area around your fireplace, the clock on your mantelpiece, the mirror in your hall. Go to the pantry for milk and a cookie and there'd be one on the cookie tin. And if you were a 1920s/30s lady, it's a fair bet that there'd be one engraved on the lid of your powder compact or your cigarette case or your lighter. And your shoes might have strips of leather arranged...you guessed. And if your local movie house is of a certain age, you never know what you might find...

1935 Alcoholics Anonymous is founded in Akron, Ohio, by ex-alcoholic Bill Wilson, 40, and his friend Dr. Robert H. Smith.

1936 An American company uses the name "Betty Crocker" to sign responses to consumer inquiries; it becomes a major brand name for many General Mills products.

1940 Former New York advertising man William Benton takes over a small company that pipes background music into restaurants and bars. It becomes known as Muzak.

artifacts and decor, in a huge range of materials from platinum to plastic. Even the most populist designs were rarely impoverished, and those who see it as a "total" design movement are dead on. And so were the Cubists, Diaghilev's Ballets Russes, and other useful sources, heavily used by Art Deco.

HEATED, LACQUERED, AND BLOWN

No, not your hair do…"High" Art Deco designs in lacquered wood, glass, and ceramics were universally admired and imitated throughout Europe and the U.S. Just look at the Chrysler Building…

Of all the "high" Art Deco craftsmen, the name of *René LALIQUE* (1860–1945) is probably the best known outside France, less because of his success as an Art Nouveau goldsmith before he neatly side-stepped into Art Deco glass manufacture, and more for his perfume bottles, car mascots, vases, clocks, and sexy ladies.

PLASTIC AND BAKELITE

Jolly stuff when you can mold it in bold, bright colors, or make it transparent. Art Deco took up new materials like plastic and Bakelite with enthusiasm: they were hard-wearing, relatively cheap, and an interesting alternative to wood. Ashtrays, napkin rings, bracelets and bangles, brooches, handbag facings: splendid stuff. Could be used large-scale for objects like radio casings, and one could incorporate that famous Art Deco sunburst.

New materials were part of the Art Deco modern esthetic, with Bakelite to the fore.

Subtle modernity: a table and stool by Jean Dunand.

1921 The Watts Towers are begun in Los Angeles by Italian-American tile-setter Simon Rodia using only hand tools, shells, glass, and other found objects.

1930 Dashiell Hammett's best-known character, the detective Sam Spade, is introduced in *The Maltese Falcon*.

1935 A record 42-pound lobster is caught off the coast of Virginia.

1910~1950

Point and Shoot
35mm photography

Paparazzi are invented.

Cameras were big, clumsy things until Kodak's Brownie (see page 48) revolutionized photography and the amateur snapshot arrived. But the quality was limited: fixed focus, with the help of a sunny day, could produce a reasonable family album picture, but not much more. Photography's next revolution, however, was around the corner, and it measured just 35 millimeters.

In the early 1910s the Leica company in Germany was commissioned to make a camera to test 35mm movie film. *Oskar BARNACK* (1879–1936), head of the research department, designed a small camera that had a good lens and took sharp pictures. It occurred to him that this would make a useful product. Following some prototype models, the Leica 1A went into production in 1924: soon it was *de rigeur* in creative circles, and 35mm quickly became a worldwide standard.

The beauty of this new hand-held camera was that it could be used in all sorts of conditions and pointed in new directions. Its small negatives could be enlarged into good-quality prints. The traditional photograph was taken from eye level, but now experimenters created new visions with bird's-eye and worm's-eye views, leading to

pictures of a dynamic impact never known before and laying the foundations of modern photojournalism. In the hands of creative photographers like Raoul Hausman, Man Ray, and Alexander Rodchenko, the photographic image was liberated. The next generation was to adopt the 35mm camera for fashion and documentary photography.

Goodbye, big black box; greetings, hand-held friend. A 1930s Leica, the camera that effectively turned photography into an art form.

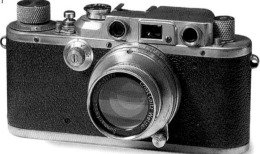

1943 Howard Hawks's film *The Outlaw* is a hit, and so is Jane Russell's cleavage, which receives more publicity than the film itself.

1945 Italians accept pea-soup powder sent to relieve hunger with reluctance, because it is so unfamiliar, but powdered eggs are universally relished.

1948 The dynamic paintings of Jackson Pollock help to launch a new school of "action painting" that will radically change the direction of American art.

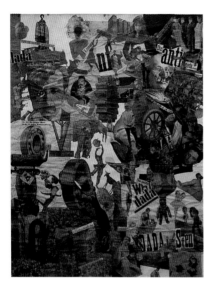

Photomontage by Hannah Höch: "Let the Dada kitchen-knife cut through the final beer-belly culture of Weimar Germany."

WHO NEEDS A CAMERA?

Fox Talbot had shown that you could record an object—ideally a flat one, like a fern—by pressing it to photographic paper and exposing it to light. The camera then took most attention for a while, but in the 1920s inventive minds returned to the camera-less photo or "photogram." *Man Ray* (1890–1976) and Dadaists like *Kurt Schwitters* (1887–1948) used its spontaneity to creative ends, with striking compositions of everyday objects. These were to have a big influence on graphic design as it broke away from nineteenth-century conformity.

YOU CAN RECYCLE

The explosion of pictorial material now in print led artists to reuse it in new combinations. *Max Ernst* (1891–1976) was the first to reconfigure nineteenth-century engravings into more sinister combinations, but *Hannah Höch* (1889–1978) led the way in seeing the potential of bizarre recombinations of photographic images: large heads on small bodies, penguins smoking cigarettes. This was photomontage, a development of collage, a visual language that was to infiltrate twentieth-century creativity, and later advertising. In the hands of left-wing designer *John Heartfield* (1891–1968), photomontage became a powerful propaganda weapon to mock the Nazis.

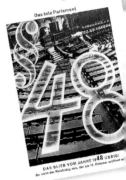

Photomontage as critical commentary: John Heartfield surveys a century of German politics.

1925 The inflation of Florida land values comes to a bad end as many investors discover the lots they have bought are underwater.

1929 The yo-yo is introduced to America by entrepreneur Donald F. Duncan; the toy is based on a weapon used by sixteenth-century Filipino hunters.

1933 Helen Jacobs is the first woman to wear shorts in lawn tennis tournament play, while the others continue to wear knee-length, or longer, skirts.

1905~1960

Infernal Combustion
Cars

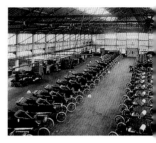

Production line: early Model Ts at Dagenham, England.

Who created the car craze? Henry FORD (1863–1947), that's who. Our Henry built his first automobile in 1896, founded his own company in 1906, introduced his famous Model T—the Tin Lizzie—to an unsuspecting planet in 1908, and became the man who "put America on four wheels," creating the greatest car-driving nation on earth. Shazaaam! By 1927, 15 million vehicles later (2 million of them in 1923 alone, amazingly), Mr. F and his imitators had created a giant industry.

The Model T was a simple and sturdy vehicle, designed and engineered for poor American roads and cross-country driving, with easily available spares (even the local blacksmith could install them) that hardly altered in twenty years. It was also the first car to be built at the rate of one per hour, using production-line methods: a large, semi-skilled labor force doing repetitive tasks.

In 1908 this little number cost a hefty $850 in any color as long as it was black; it became cheaper in time, mainly because the basic design stayed more or less unchanged. But as roads everywhere became better, an enthusiastic public hungered for improved engineering and appearance. There would be trouble ahead…

Nice day out
The Austin 7 and other popular models helped to advance the cause of tourism, thanks to fresh ideas about leisure that appeared increasingly in magazines and in advertising campaigns run by petroleum companies. You—and your car—could be sure with Shell (or so the posters said).

The much-loved Morris Traveller—station-wagon version of the Minor—was introduced in 1953.

1944 Carbon monoxide fumes kill more than 100 Italians in a rail tunnel near Balvano. The victims are mostly black-market operators trading in eggs, meat, and olive oil.

1959 The Treaty of Rome creates the European Economic Community.

1960 An earthquake near Concepción, Chile, creates seismic waves that shatter many coastal towns, traveling to Hilo, Hawaii, and eventually reaching as far as Japan.

MEANWHILE, ACROSS THE POND, IN A DIFFERENT WORLD...

...*Herbert AUSTIN* (1866–1941), English farmer's son turned inventive engineer, was also interested in production lines. Austin built his first car in Birmingham in 1905, to keep his workforce employed, and didn't look back. Nor did his competitor *William R. MORRIS* (1877–1963; absolutely no relation to the Arts and Crafts guru), who opened his factory at Cowley, near Oxford.

Both companies learned from Ford. Their aims—affordable vehicles, comfortable and cheap to run ("motoring at tram fares," someone called it)—ran parallel for decades, until they merged in 1951. In 1922 Austin produced the Austin 7 (a.k.a the

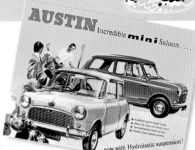

The Mini, as much a 1960s British icon as that other mini.

Mighty Mini or "the bed pan"), Britain's answer to the Tin Lizzie. It was meant to be a true family car, and at £200 it was cheap: a four-seater with leather upholstery, room for two kids in the back and Mom and Dad up front, a diddly 696cc engine in the basic model, and hardly any design changes until 1939. Three hundred thousand were sold, and helped to spread auto-mania in Britain.

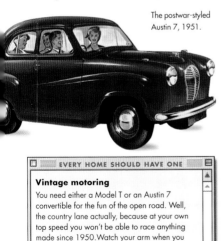

The postwar-styled Austin 7, 1951.

EVERY HOME SHOULD HAVE ONE

Vintage motoring

You need either a Model T or an Austin 7 convertible for the fun of the open road. Well, the country lane actually, because at your own top speed you won't be able to race anything made since 1950. Watch your arm when you turn the crank, and beware: these creatures are addictive and serious money-guzzlers.

All mod cons?

World War I caused most commercial car design outside the U.S. to cease. Afterward, it began again with a vengeance everywhere, but though big companies like Ford, Fiat, Austin, and Renault grew, standardized mechanical design took a little longer. Refinements like four-wheel braking, centralized gear levers, and the widespread adoption of pneumatic tires were creature comforts for drivers that evolved only from the mid-1920s.

In the 1950s, British design too often lacked the enterprise, imagination, and color of the Americans, and Ford and General Motors triumphed with American streamlining. Even Morris's popular Minor 1000 could not totally overcome the allure of Ford's shark's-fin paint-and-chrome. Rock'n'roll was here to stay.

1931 German film *Mädchen in Uniform* (*Girls in Uniform*) is the first film to portray lesbian love.

1937 Barcelona physician Jose Trutta Raspall introduces a closed-plaster method of treatment to save fracture victims in the Spanish Civil War and reduce the need for amputation.

1941 A BBC broadcast from London urges the subjugated peoples of Europe to whistle the opening motif of Beethoven's Symphony No. 5 whenever Nazi soldiers are around.

1920~1960

Any Shape as Long as It's Geometric
Bauhaus

With De Stijl and Constructivism, the Bauhaus was and is one of the most influential sources of modern design—arguably the most influential, though there are skeptics now just as there were then. But unlike the first two, the Bauhaus was a real design school, with real pupils and a star-studded staff. Born in Weimar, Germany, in 1919, it died one death in Berlin in 1933 and was later partly reborn in the United States.

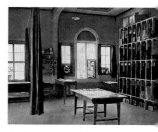

The glass-painting studio at the Bauhaus, 1923.

Literally and lumpishly translated as "construction house," the Bauhaus has an interesting story. It was established by architect *Walter Gropius* (1883–1969), a man who saw himself as a machine-age successor of Chairman William Morris, and whose twin

Bauhaus Cabinet meeting, c.1927: Gropius and Co. on the roof of the Dessau Bauhaus.

ideals were (simply put) "truth to material" and "form follows function." Lost already? The material used to make an object should be appropriate for its purpose. Form should be modern, abstract, and functional, with universal appeal, liberated from historical references. So, goodbye, Antiquity.

Gropius merged the two Weimar art schools and hired a great team to educate his students in a tuition system where craftsmanship, art, and architecture overlapped. Result? Super-craftsmen, *natürlich*. Well…good all-rounders, anyway, taught by the likes of Paul Klee, Wassily Kandinsky, and László Moholy-Nagy.

1946 The first postwar bananas go on sale in London's Covent Garden Market.

1955 A contract between American Can and Continental Can on August 13 wins United Steel Workers the first 52-week guaranteed annual wage in any major U.S. industry.

1959 Saudi Arabia's King Faisal agrees to education for girls despite protests from some religious groups.

EVERY HOME SHOULD HAVE ONE

A Wassily chair

Designed in 1925 by Marcel Breuer and named after the famous Russian artist and Bauhaus tutor Wassily Kandinsky, this is a seriously good example of the combination of tubular steel and leather. If you can afford one, or find a copy that's well made, go for it. But once you're sitting, don't try to get up quickly.

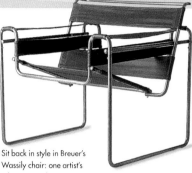

Sit back in style in Breuer's Wassily chair: one artist's tribute to another.

Although philosophical arguments threatened the school (Herr G himself left in 1928), the Bauhaus survived to move in 1926 to Dessau for its most famous, modern, purpose-built incarnation. In 1932 the Dessau site was closed by the Nazis (the charge was "cultural Bolshevism"), but staggered on to Berlin, where it finally collapsed in 1933.

BUT FOR THE BAUHAUS...

...there'd be no nice modern typography. *Herbert B*AYER (1900–85) invented a universal type in 1925, a sans-serif alphabet based on curves and straight lines. It was revised in 1928, and its variants are everywhere— and on your PC, too.

And there'd be no Josef Albers and Johannes Itten to give today's artists and designers a decent scientific color theory. And none of those Bauhaus designs that just won't die, like Marcel Breuer's chairs with tubular steel frames, which gave hope to legions of brain-dead imitators, or the metalwork utensils, from ashtrays and table lamps to coffeepots, of Marianne Brandt, whose class and taste kicked ass in a man's world.

Silver and bronze ashtray by Marianne Brandt, 1923–4.

DESIGNER NAMES

The 1920s and 30s saw the emergence of women designers, usually underpaid and often sidelined by employers for purely sexist reasons. **Marianne Brandt** *(1893–1984) entered the Bauhaus in 1923, learned the geometry of Constructivist esthetics from Moholy-Nagy, and became one of the most important Bauhaus designers. Her tea and coffee set of 1924, made with mass production in mind, is now a classic of modern design, relaunched by the Italian Alessi company in 1985. Brandt's lamps and light fixtures were simple, functional, and inspirational; someone you know owns a descendant.*

1903 German Rheinhold Burger patents the Thermos flask, which had been invented, but not patented, by Scottish scientist James Dewar in 1892.

1909 Standard Oil Company head and the world's first billionaire, John D. Rockefeller, gives $530 million for worldwide medical research.

$530m

1927 Fritz Lang directs *Metropolis*. The film costs five million marks and takes 11 months to make.

1890~1940

Electric Lines
The London Underground

Cities had become the nerve centers of civilization in the nineteenth century. Cities were where things happened. They were the hothouses of culture, where new ideas were plotted and carried out. The avant-garde had its birth in Paris before the 1890s—literature, theater, music, design, and the visual arts were revolutionized. Cities had always been the centers of commerce, banking, and trading. The department store arrived to tempt more people into town. So, efficient systems for getting commuters and shoppers from the suburbs and back again were needed.

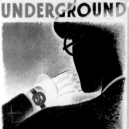

No idle boast, because the London Underground in the 1930s was a transport of delight (as well as being splendidly illustrated).

Technology played a leading part in this, as the horse-drawn bus gave way to the motor bus and the electric tram. In competition were the railroads. The pioneering London Metropolitan Railway of 1863 ran partly on the surface and partly in tunnels, but steam and smoke were a particular disadvantage in the underground sections. Then electric trains started in the 1890s, and underground railroads became a real possibility. In London the system expanded to serve the whole city, and it became a model copied the world over.

YOU'RE MY TYPE
In 1915 *Edward JOHNSTON* (1874–1944), a calligrapher, was commissioned to design a new typeface for the unified London Underground system. The man behind this was *Frank PICK* (1878–1941), the operational director of London Transport.

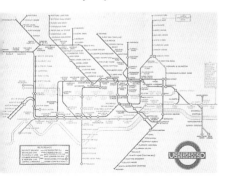

A cartographic classic from 1931, and perhaps the most regularly consulted map.

1931 Rickenbacker transforms popular music by introducing the electric guitar: "Frying Pan" steel guitar and "Electro Spanish" are two of the firm's most popular models.

1934 *Le Jazz Hot* by French critic Hugues Panassié is the first book of jazz criticism to be published.

1939 American chemist Bradley Dewey opens a pilot plant for making synthetic rubber.

EVERY HOME SHOULD HAVE ONE

Marx on the seat

Or every train at least. A major contribution to the Underground style came from Enid Marx *(see page 76)*, with her designs for seating fabric for London Transport's buses and trains. For nearly forty years from 1937, generations of Londoners proved the resilience of these bold, hard-wearing patterns—by sitting on them.

Pick imposed a regime of modernity and unified design principles on the Underground system, and saw himself as an evangelizing crusader who would encourage the public to appreciate good design through its efficiency.

By the 1930s the system was the envy of the world—modernistic stations, sleek, efficient trains, and passengers guided by Harry BECK's (1903–74) original concept for a new type of diagrammatic map. The revolutionary simple modern typeface and roundel logo that Johnston designed are still in use today, and inspired others. In Germany *Paul RENNER* (1878–1956) created Futura (1925), while in England *Eric GILL* (1882–1940) was responsible for Gill Sans. These were clean-cut modern typefaces for the electric age.

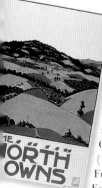

The scent of fresh air, given to Londoners in 1916 by E. McKnight Kauffer.

POSTER LIBERATION

It wasn't just typefaces that changed. A new generation of poster designers, inspired by Cubism and abstraction, revitalized the billboards in the "Tube" stations. *E. McKnight KAUFFER* (1890–1954), *Tom PURVIS* (1888–1959), and *Frank NEWBOULD* (1887–1951) showed the public that modern art wasn't confined to the gallery.

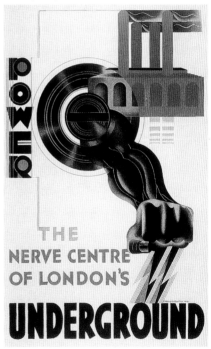

Kauffer again, this time from the 1930s. The genteel pastoral has given way to a more arresting modernist-symbolist style.

1929 The first crease-resistant cotton fabric is developed by Tootal's of St. Helens, England.

1934 Atatürk (Mustafa Kemal) grants Turkish women the right to vote.

1935 In the U.S., the Works Progress Administration creates jobs for artists in a project to decorate post offices and other federal buildings.

1920~1945

Household Affairs
Modernity penetrates the home

Tea with Clarice Cliff.

Even though women were the key consumers, design had been dominated by the male half of the species for most of its history. By the 1920s women began to get in on the act, especially in interior design, furniture, carpets, and fabrics. The modern look came to the home as geometry and new materials took over from stuffy Edwardian styles. Ideas began to spread from the Bauhaus and the De Stijl group into well-heeled homes. Exhibitions, especially the 1924 Paris Exhibition, had a dramatic impact through magazines like Vogue *and* Harper's Bazaar.

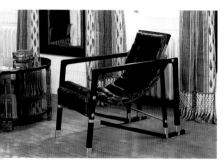

The Transat, a leather chair with black lacquered frame by Eileen Gray, c. 1930.

EILEEN GRAY

An outstanding example was *Eileen GRAY* (1878–1975), a Scottish-Irish artist-architect-craftswoman who excelled in the new Zeitgeist. Her designs combined modernity with the old Arts and Crafts dictum: truth to materials. She could lacquer like a Japanese craftsman, her understanding of space was excellent, and her minimalist geometric glass and steel tables are still in production today.

DESIGNER NAMES

With **Enid Marx** *(1902–99) the concepts of modernity and style contrast interestingly with the work of the Bauhaus's Marianne Brandt (see page 73). At London's Royal College of Art (1922–25), Marx was inspired by a new wave of wood engravers to develop hand-block decoration of fabrics into a fine art, using modernist, abstract patterns. A major figure by 1939, she patterned British "Utility" garments (1944–45) and then just carried on: postage stamps, book jackets, and wrapping paper all received the benefits of her talent.*

DESIGNER NAMES

1942 In the U.S., "Chattanooga Choo Choo," voted tune of the year in 1941, is awarded the first-ever gold disk after selling a million copies.

1943 The richest Americans eat five pounds of cheese a week, while the poor have less than one pound.

1945 The U.S. Mint uses salvaged shell casings to press into coins.

ON A PLATE

Women designers made a major contribution to the ceramics industry in Britain. Pottery was one of the first mass-produced items, but modernized very slowly. Even with new industrial techniques, much handwork had to be done, and women were usually the decorators.

A startling talent was that of *Susie COOPER* (1902–95), who began as a decorator but started designing from 1923 and subsequently produced a prolific flow of designs for household pottery, both functional and decorative. Her designs reflected the changing tastes of a long career, during which she designed thousands of shapes and patterns.

More memorable were the jazz-age designs of her contemporary *Clarice CLIFF* (1899–1972), who had

Lose your cuffs

…was what British men did when they wore Utility clothing. Introduced in 1942 by Hugh Dalton, the Utility scheme was a development of the public rationing imposed by the British government from 1940 on. Utility aimed to economize on raw materials by imposing design solutions on everything from cloth through dishes to furniture and back again. The concept of designing for austerity was interesting: self-respect without frills, especially for people who had been bombed out of their homes, or newlyweds. It improved after 1945 and died after 1950, but oh, those noisy steel-framed beds.

a huge success in the late 1920s with her "Bizarre" line, which is as big now as it was then. Cliff's patterns were simple and geometric, her colors blindingly bright and unforgettable. Both women established their own pottery companies.

Reflecting the geometry of the Bauhaus and the machine age, Margarete Marks

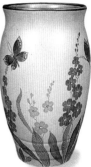

1938 vase by Susie Cooper, a typical example of her decorative style.

designed a starkly modern tea set for Ridgeway in 1930. With changes in taste, Hungarian Eva Zeisel's 1942 dinner service design "Museum" for Shenango in the U.S. was white porcelain, completely undecorated, with soft, curving lines.

Clarice Cliff jazzed up tea with some unfamiliar angles.

1934 U.S. prison bureau buys the island of Alcatraz in San Francisco Bay as a site for a new prison.

1937 In Britain, cartons of Lyons coffee become the first product to carry a sell-by date.

1955 The Vienna State Opera House reopens after having been almost totally destroyed by wartime bombing and gunfire.

1920~1970

Making Machines for Living In
Le Corbusier and others

Le Corbusier.

From abstract to concrete, LE CORBUSIER (a.k.a. Charles Édouard Jeanneret, 1887–1965) gets into all the books. But which Le Corbusier do you want? The architect-cum-designer who pushed the idea of "less is more" (he wasn't the only one); who famously wrote in his book Towards a New Architecture *(1923) that a house was "...a machine for living in"? The guy whose ideas about order, simplicity, and function cemented (sorry) the development of the concrete high-rise apartment building in Western Europe? Or Le Corbusier the 1920s design theorist, rejecting florid nineteenth-century ornament, pioneer of the "Engineer's Aesthetic"?*

That purity and undecorated form, those open, divisible interiors, the need for factory-made, utilitarian objects? Did he read it in an issue of *De Stijl*? It all smacks of a large slug of Bauhaus with a Rietveld chaser, and it's interesting that Le Corbusier caught the design bug in the decade 1920–30, when De Stijl and the Bauhaus were so prominent in Europe. What's different about Le Corbusier's ideas at this time is his determination to integrate design into architecture.

WHAT'S INSIDE?

Le Corbu differed from the rest because he physically integrated furniture into his buildings as part of the design. Objects weren't just constructed to harmonize with the overall feel of a room: they were actually part of the architecture itself. Concrete dining table, Madam? *Absolument!*

A skeletal chaise longue frame designed by Le Corbusier and Charlotte Perriand, 1928.

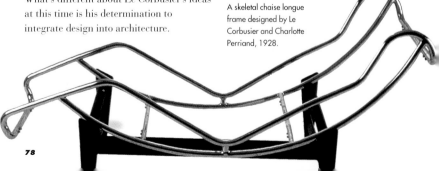

1957 Dr. Seuss writes children's favorite *The Cat in the Hat*.

1960 Aluminum cans are used commercially for the first time for food and beverages; this will come to be the single largest use of aluminum.

1963 Chairman Mao's "little red book" of quotations is published, despite the fact that he claims "to read too many books is harmful."

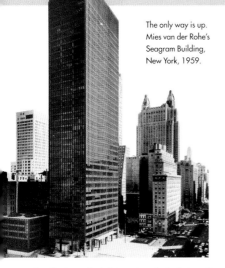

The only way is up. Mies van der Rohe's Seagram Building, New York, 1959.

DESIGNER NAMES

Ludwig Mies van der Rohe
(1886–1969) was born into a family of Aachen stonemasons. The last Bauhaus director (Berlin, 1932–33), Mies took the school to Chicago in 1938 and became one of the century's great architects, a design Führer in glass and steel. But Mies's fame as the Windy City's skyscraper innovator didn't stop him from also making great chairs. Cool, elegant, curvy ones, different from Breuer's. The cantilevered Barcelona (1929), the Tugendhat (1929–30), the Brno (1930). Not for mass production: too much finesse. But great, just the same. And, like Breuer's, they're still around.

DESIGNER NAMES

Le Corbu called this rationale "efficient," but the best of his deluxe designs for furnishings, made during 1928–29 with his assistant *Charlotte Perriand* (b.1903), weren't easily mass-produced. Designer objects like the Grand Confort club armchair and the B306 chaise longue have complete snob value—but the furniture of *Marcel Breuer* (1902–81) is better known. A Hungarian Bauhaus student, Breuer was successful by 1930 on the strength of his innovations in furniture design using tubular steel (it's said he was inspired by his bike!). Breuer's club chair of 1925 headed a steadily evolving series of simple, steel-framed furniture.

At the Bauhaus, in Europe, in Britain in 1935–37, and then in the U.S., Breuer refined his designs, experimenting with other metals and with wood and plywood. They're still being copied, which shows how good they were to start with.

Simple: a Mies chair from 1929, a variation on the cantilever theme.

EVERY HOME SHOULD HAVE ONE

Barcelona

...one of Mies van der Rohe's Barcelona chairs, for the same reason that you should have a Wassily: they're just too comfortable. All the same, once you have one, you'll be just another couch potato.

1827 English chemist John Walker invents the "Lucifer," the first friction match; its head is made of potash, sugar, and gum arabic.

1848 Spain's Seville Fair has its beginnings in an April cattle market that will grow to become a six-day event and one of the major fairs in Europe.

1895 Oscar Wilde is convicted of homosexuality and sentenced to two years' hard labor.

1820~1940

Rubber Gloves to Plastic Raincoats
Synthetics

Staying out of the rain.

Natural resources have been devastated by humans for as long as we have needed materials to make things. So what happens when we run out? We have to find or invent substitutes. As early as the 1880s, the enormous demand for ivory to make chessmen, furniture, piano keys, and (particularly) billiard balls was devastating the world's elephant population. Even then, it was clear that alternatives would have to be found.

The first "plastics" were derived from natural products that were modified chemically to become more useful. In the 1820s a Scottish entrepreneur had made liquid rubber and treated fabric with it to make it waterproof. His name: Macintosh —and thus the raincoat was born. Other natural rubbery substances were seized upon to fulfill new technological needs, such as gutta percha, used in 1850 to insulate the first underwater cable between England and France.

DESIGNER NAMES

In the United States, struggling inventor **Charles Goodyear** *(1800–60) discovered the possibility of adding sulfur to raw rubber, converting it into a useful material— "vegetable leather," he called it. He designed dozens of rubber products— canoes, pants, air valves, musical instruments, and inflatable furniture—which were shown at the 1851 Great Exhibition.*

DESIGNER NAMES

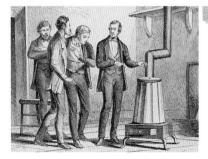

No, you can't drink it. Charles Goodyear demonstrates his discovery of rubber.

Various European chemists had been playing around with cellulose, treating it with acids that produced a violent explosive. It could also be mixed with ether and alcohol to make a clear lacquer. This transformed photography when

1911 Albert I of the Belgians grants Lever Brothers a Belgian Congo concession to plant oil palms to create oils for his soaps and margarines on condition that they pay minimum wages and establish schools and hospitals.

1921 English explorers find tracks like huge human footprints in the Himalayas, and the yeti legend is born.

1927 The first transatlantic telephone call takes place at a cost of $75, half the price of a car.

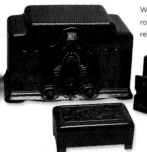

Wondrous Bakelite, robust, versatile, reliable, and cheap.

it could be stamped and molded, two crucial machine processes that speeded up production. Soon thousands of artifacts, from dolls' faces to bicycle mudguards, would be made of it.

THE WONDER STUFF

The first synthetic plastic—Bakelite—was patented in 1907 by Belgian-American inventor *Leo BAEKELAND* (1863–1944). It could be molded into permanent shapes, determining what it was possible to design and mass produce. It also had good electrical properties, which led it to be widely used in the radio industry. A pioneer in this field was Ekco in Britain, who commissioned designs from architects like *Wells COATES* (1895–1958).

sculptor *Frederick Scott ARCHER* (1813–57) used it to coat photographic plates, improving their sensitivity. British inventor *Alexander PARKES* (1813–90) was one of the first to convert it into a practical material by adding binders and colorants. He exhibited a variety of objects at the Great International Exhibition of 1862—walking canes, picture frames, knife and fork handles, and combs—but his business failed.

It fell to *John HYATT* (1837–1920) in the U.S. to perfect a useful material, initially used to make dental plates and shirt collars, which he named "celluloid." Despite its shortcomings (it warped when heated and was highly flammable),

EVERY HOME SHOULD HAVE ONE

Show a leg

The Du Pont Company had made large profits from munitions in World War I, and embarked on a massive research program to make an improved synthetic fiber. This work blossomed when research scientist Wallace Carothers perfected nylon in 1931. By the end of the decade, the most desirable product for the fashionable young woman was a pair of ... nylons.

Sheer bliss: a shapely case made for nylon.

1931 Miles Laboratories of Elkhart, Indiana, introduces the antacid analgesic tablet Alka-Seltzer.

1931 U.S. cinemas show double features to boost business; many unemployed executives spend their afternoons at the pictures.

1935 British inventor A. Edwin Stevens produces the first wearable electronic hearing aid and founds a company he calls Amplivox to produce the two-pound device.

1930~1940

After the Crash

1930s developments

Everything was going so well, and then … 1929, the bubble burst. The good times were not going to last forever. The jazz-age boom ground to an abrupt stop with the Wall Street crash. The loss of confidence, the calling in of loans, had a worldwide effect as the Depression set in. Despite its enormous wealth, the U.S. suffered as much as other countries. Incomes and prices fell, and consumer demand evaporated. How could the economy be revived?

The classic 30s telephone, designed by Jean Heiberg for Ericsson of Sweden.

One way of restoring sales was to make products more desirable: more attractive, fitting the age. A brand of new talent emerged to do this—and a new type of professional, the design consultant.

One of the first to establish himself, separately from architects or engineers, was *Walter Dorwin TEAGUE* (1883–1960), a graphic designer who established a product-design consultancy in 1926. His first big client was Kodak, for whom he designed the Art Deco Vanity in 1928 and the streamlined Bantam Special in 1936. *Henry DREYFUSS* (1904–72) created the classic 300 desk telephone for Bell in 1937 and continued to design phones for them through his career. Public confidence grew as

products became more desirable, and during the 30s the U.S. economy boomed.

This was the go-faster decade—and nothing expressed this better than streamlining. Aerodynamicists had found that the teardrop shape reduced wind resistance in fast-moving objects. Austrian designer-engineer *Paul JARAY* (1889–1974) applied the principle to giant airships, and a 1933 body for a Mercedes 200 was way ahead of its time.

Is it a plane? Strangely, no, it's a car: Buckminster Fuller's Dymaxion of 1933.

1936 Black American Jesse Owens wins the 100m Gold Medal at the Berlin Olympics.

1938 New York enacts the first state law requiring medical tests for marriage license applicants.

1940 New York surgeon Charles Richard Drew opens the first blood bank, but segregation rules prevent him from donating his own blood.

DESIGNER NAMES

Raymond Loewy *(1893–1986) was to become one of the first famous designers—apart from fashion designers, that is. An immigrant from France, he started as an advertising illustrator, but then was asked to redesign a Gestetner duplicating machine in 1929. His 1932 redesign of the Coldspot refrigerator for Sears Roebuck dramatically boosted its sales, and he quickly became an established design consultant. This was the first fridge to borrow from car production, with a flush white pressed-steel frame and door, and the "this year's model" approach.*

inspirational. Geddes, together with *Raymond LOEWY* (1893–1986), Teague, and Dreyfuss, were the main designers for the futuristic exhibits in the New York World's Fair of 1939, which attempted to predict the America of the 1960s.

Major pavilions were sponsored by the likes of Ford and General Motors, where visitors could see wonderful new systems for car drivers and pedestrians (walkways for the latter). Sparky the Robot in the Westinghouse exhibit showed that a brave new world lay ahead. What the exhibition ignored was the imminent arrival of World War II.

Family firm

Rarely has one family made such an impact as the Castiglionis. Livio (1911–79) and Pier (1913–68) set up in 1938, making their mark with the 1940 Phonola radio. They were joined by Achille (b. 1918). Their versatile designs helped establish Italy's reputation for innovation with furniture, lighting, and interiors.

THE FUTURE STARTS HERE

Visionary designer *Norman BEL GEDDES* (1893–1958) was an unparalleled communicator of advanced design ideas. Although few were realized, his streamlined designs for cars, buses, ocean liners, and flying boats in his book *Horizons* (1932) were

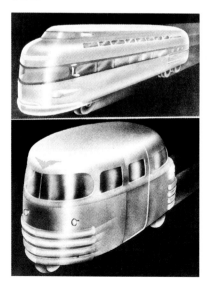

Futuristic designs by Raymond Loewy for a bus and a taxi. These were among many ideas exhibited at the 1939 New York World's Fair.

1933 The influenza virus is isolated for the first time following an epidemic in London.

1942 The T-shirt is devised by the U.S. Navy and fast becomes a popular streetwear fashion item.

1943 At Bletchley Park, UK, an electronic machine called Colossus is developed to crack coded messages, and proves that computers can be more than simply machines to manipulate numbers.

1930~1970

Simple Is as Simple Does
Beetle and Jeep: wartime classics

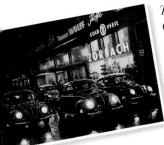

Two of the oddest classic car stories are the German Volkswagen Beetle and the American Willys-Overland Jeep. Both were designed for easy construction and mass production, and while few Beetles were made before the end of World War II, the Jeep was a real War Baby.

On your marks… Volkswagen Beetles commanding the city streets in 1953.

As for VW, the KdF Wagen (or "Strength through joy car": yes, really) was the result of a 1933 agreement between Ferdinand Porsche and the motorbike companies NSU and Zundapp for a small car. The German government put one foot in the door, and Porsche's first VW appeared in 1934 as a rear-engined, air-cooled sedan. Just right for the Autobahns—terrestrial superhighways, designed and built by the Nazis to combat German unemployment.

Post-1945, with VW under British control, the car went into volume production at Wolfsburg. In 1949 VW reverted to German control and never looked back. Nicknamed the Beetle, it did phenomenal business in the U.S., where buyers wanted a cheap, well-designed and -engineered small car. In the 1960s, the Beetle received a series of new engines and

designs, but by 1974 it was old hat. The Beetle is dead; long live the Golf. But wait: when you read this, Beetle sales are in excess of 21 million, and VW gave the car a full makeover and a relaunch in 1998.

Why Jeep?
According to some, the Jeep was originally called the "Peep" for reasons unknown. "Jeep" stuck, a shortening of GP: General Purpose. Like Swalk. And Snafu.

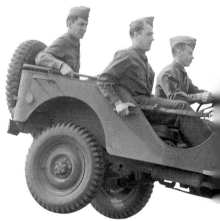

1949 Pope Pius XII excommunicates all communists from the Roman Catholic Church.

1955 Movie star Marilyn Monroe is given a bigger, better contract by Fox; they will not only give her $100,000 for each film, but also a cut of the profits and script and director approval.

1970 Earth Day in the U.S. brings the first mass demonstrations against pollution and other desecrations of the planet's ecology in an attempt to raise awareness.

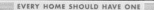

☐ ▤ EVERY HOME SHOULD HAVE ONE ▤ ▤

Classic pair

One of each, in fact. It doesn't matter whether the VW was made on license somewhere: it'll be fine because it is what it is. As for the Jeep, you need the battle-dress to go with it, and the bank balance to take care of the gas, but when you've dealt with these details, you'll be the envy of all who see you. Don't forget to take the helmet off when you go into the bank.

PEEP PEEP

The Jeep was simply the first off-road vehicle. The Military Model MB Jeep began to roll off American production lines in 1940, intended as a multipurpose workhorse, an open vehicle, compact, solid, and with tire treads deep enough to take nearly any terrain. They were expendable, too: wartime production ran at 40 vehicles per hour! Mechanically simple, with a four-cylinder engine that could run at 4,000 rpm for hours, it could take six passengers or heavy loads, tilt at alarming angles, and still keep going.

This was good, because Jeeps served as gun-mountings for a wide variety of light artillery, as fuel carriers, ambulances, and communications vehicles, and rarely complained. When

It even flies! A U.S. Army Jeep takes to the air.

the war ended, everyone wanted one. That was OK: there were lots to go around, and they kept on coming until 1970. Chrysler bought the name in 1985, and their Jeep is…well, a little more refined. No thrills.

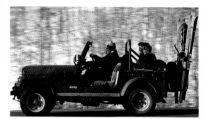

The contemporary peacetime Jeep, loaded down as usual, but this time with all the accoutrements of a ski party instead of machine guns.

DESIGNER NAMES

Say it directly. Don't mince words. **Abram Games** *(1914–98) and* **Frank Newbould** *(1887–1951) delivered some memorable pictorial and patriotic messages to the British public from 1940–45, and were arguably the best British graphic designers of World War II. Their American counterparts were employed by the Office of War Information and included the great* **Norman Rockwell** *(1894–1978), whose "Four Freedoms" and powerful "Let's give him enough and on time" had an urgency that the British don't often match.*

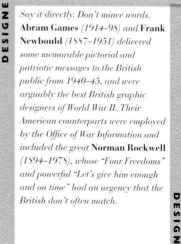

1946 Jackie Robinson is the first black man to play major league baseball in the U.S.

1947 Britain nationalizes electricity production by forming an Electricity Authority that takes over 550 private electric companies.

1950 Otis Elevators installs the first passenger elevators with self-opening doors in the Atlantic Refining building in Dallas.

1945~1960

Pick Yourself Up, Dust Yourself Off

Postwar revival

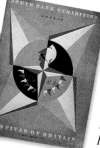

The Festival of Britain catalog, with its neat logo.

After 1945 the only way was up: surely humans could sink no lower? Designers, as much as anyone, looked for new hope. Some developments had been in the pipeline pre-1939; others were new and short-term. One of the latter—big for its time—was the Festival of Britain, best known for the exhibition held in London in 1951 on a 27-acre bomb site by the River Thames.

L ondon's centenary nod to the Great Exhibition of 1851, it was an inducement to visitors to come to town, (a) to lighten up after a long war, (b) to remind themselves about British achievements in design and technology, and (c) to imagine the future, bursting with new ideas and inventions. Don't be cynical: it was important. Kids of the 1950s who went say it was all a bit too earnest-minded, but a great experience.

ARRIVA ITALIA

In Europe, Italy's big moment finally arrived: a long moment, too, and designers like *Marcello NIZZOLI* (1887–1969) and *Corradino D'ASCANIO* (1891–1981) signaled things to come. Nizzoli was an Italian version of Gerrit Rietveld; and like

The joy of scootering, Vespa-style.

GR, Nizzoli was at his best when he was messing about with things. He messed about with Olivetti from 1920, not only giving the company (wait for it) a corporate image, but also presenting the world with some cool, streamlined business gear. Only Thor would thunder through a letter on an Adler typewriter: Nizzoli's designs for Olivetti changed life in the office forever.

And d'Ascanio is the man every self-respecting British modernist thanks for designing the Vespa motor scooter for Piaggio. They began production in 1946,

1954 A Supreme Court judgment outlaws segregation in American schools.

1957 A high-speed (350,000 rpm) dental drill devised by American dentist John V. Borden reduces the time needed for each patient and is less painful.

1958 In Paris, Yves Saint-Laurent holds his first-ever fashion show.

but were soon rivaled by Lambretta from 1947, and both brands quickly caught on across Europe, where the flatulent sound of their engines was music to teenage ears.

DESIGNER NAMES

Marcello Nizzoli was 53 when he began to design in earnest. As a textile and exhibition designer before that, he'd had a flair for reinventing things. His redesign package for Necchi sewing machines is an object lesson in changing a fusty image to a modern, sophisticated one. He had this ability in common with Sixten Sason and Ernest Race; all three had strong ideas about what we'd call "lifestyle" and "contemporary" and "sophistication."

DESIGNER NAMES

Domes of discovery

The Festival of Britain set the pattern for spendthrift exhibition design. For a country so short of raw materials in 1951 and whose industry was so hard-pressed, British politicians behaved abominably by systematically trashing the site at the end of the show. Of the 1951 bash, only the Royal Festival Hall remains. We wouldn't do that now, would we? Well…the futuristic Dome of Discovery, so loved by Festival of Britain crowds, was reincarnated in 1999, in slightly different form, at Greenwich, in honor of the new millennium. After the party's over, unless a buyer can be found, it seems that this, too, might be reduced to waste. It defies description. First waste public money; then waste it again.

IT'S SMOOTH! IT'S SAAB!

Meanwhile in the chilly north, two near-contemporaries with aviation backgrounds used their knowledge for different ends. Sweden's designer-for-hire (and highly regarded) *Sixten Sason* (1912–69) presented SAAB aviation (then new to the auto industry) with a one-piece, welded-steel monocoque streamlined teardrop of a car in 1946. Was it a plane? Nearly. SAAB modified it, called it the 92, and it ran virtually unchanged for 35 years. It was Sason's best-known design.

In Britain, *Ernest Race* (1913–64) began a furniture design and manufacturing business. Wood was very scarce, so Race decided to make chairs from scrap metal instead. Reconditioned aluminum made strong, light, modern furniture that wasn't tied to a design group's manifesto. Presto: success.

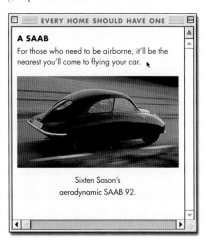

EVERY HOME SHOULD HAVE ONE

A SAAB

For those who need to be airborne, it'll be the nearest you'll come to flying your car.

Sixten Sason's aerodynamic SAAB 92.

1943 American big band leader Glenn Miller mysteriously disappears on a flight from England to France, and is never seen again.

1954 In the U.S., Bell Telecommunications designs the first practical solar battery.

1963 Cigar smokers in the U.S. are badly hit by President Kennedy's total ban on trade with Cuba.

1920~1960

Like a Bird in the Sky
Air travel

The Boeing Stratocruiser, flagship of BOAC's transatlantic fleet.

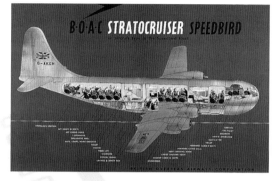

Remember that ghastly, serpentine check-in line at JFK, Heathrow, O'Hare, Tel-Aviv, or wherever; and how we curse and ask ourselves how things ever reached such a pretty pass? It was so much simpler in the 1920s, when all air travel was a luxury affair, and "economy class" was…different! Then, old World War I bombers were converted for passenger use, but we're talking about twos and threes, and sometimes the passengers had to wear flying suits. A better bet, circa 1919–20, was the French Farman Goliath F60 biplane, which could get you and 11 friends to your destination (as long as it was within 250 miles) at 75 mph. Oh, my.

Come fly with us
Eventually, flights were energetically advertised by a series of excellent posters by top designers, using a combination of photography and modern typography. For the purely modern art purists, the painter Ben Nicholson (1894–1982) designed Imperial's famous Speedbird motif, a zigzag figure that went on to represent BOAC into the 1960s.

Britain's Imperial Airways was one of Europe's most interesting and exciting success stories in the early interwar years. Imperial's all-metal de Havilland DH66 Hercules three-engined biplanes were a familiar sight at Croydon Airport, south of London. In a Hercules, with six companions, you could begin an odyssey that ended in India at a cruising speed of 110 mph. In time—in one of Imperial's Handley Page HP42s—you could end up anywhere in Europe, along with 20 new friends. And if travelers wanted luxury and romance, they could fly south in 750-mile stages in an Imperial flying boat built by Short Brothers of Belfast. Or with Germany's Dornier boats. Or France's Latecoere or Breguet.

1963 In Britain, 15 masked men steal over £2.5 million in the "Great Train Robbery," a daring raid on the Scotland-to-London Post Office Express.

1966 British entrepreneur Freddie Laker forms Laker Airways, an airline company specializing in budget vacations.

1969 Bad boy actor-director Dennis Hopper finally wins the approval of the studios with his hippie-biker hit *Easy Rider*.

SIMPLY THE BEST

The great aircraft success story of the 1930s was the DC3, a brilliant, streamlined low-wing monoplane aircraft, designed by *Arthur Raymond* (1889–1999), which first flew for Douglas in 1935, went on to put America in touch with itself, and is still flying. Versatility was its name: it has carried passengers, parcels, paratroopers, and more. Raymond said that it was "a little like the Model-T Ford." Such modesty: it was better.

The DC3 was a variant of Douglas's DC2, built to carry the U.S. mail, in competition with Boeing's 221 Monomail. When it came in second in an England–Australia air race in 1934, with a payload of cargo and full crew, against a designed de Havilland racing plane, various minds were blown. The DC3 entered service with American Airlines in 1936, and it hasn't stopped going, at home and abroad.

APRÈS LA GUERRE

In Britain, raw materials were so scant that the aviation industry used converted bombers. Avro Lancasters became Lancastrians (when they weren't Yorks). In the U.S. they did much the same: Boeing's Stratocruiser (introduced 1948) was just an inflated military airplane with decent food, but it answered the demand for

Jetting into the future

Well, perhaps not every home...Britain's de Havilland DH6 Comet was a pioneering aircraft and a design-conscious one, too. The Comet made the first jet passenger flight from London to Johannesburg in 1952, but the square windows of its early versions made it accident-prone, despite its beautiful wing-rooted engines. Oval windows appeared, and all was well...too late. The nasty external, wing-mounted engine pods of Boeing's 707 and later variants did what the Comet should have done, and took more passengers farther, on more routes, in the 1960s and 70s, than ever before.

EVERY HOME SHOULD HAVE ONE

long-haul aircraft. Ditto Lockheed's Constellation series, a.k.a. the C69, with its triple tail fins—an inspiration to schoolboys around the globe. But the biggest leap was made by Douglas (again), who—in a couple of hops—brought out the DC7, which could jump the North Atlantic in one leap.

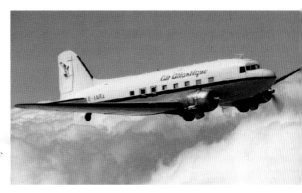

The DC3, designed by Arthur Raymond: airborne star of the 1930s.

1940 The first nylon stockings go on sale in the U.S.; they will not be available in Britain until 1946.

1947 The Edinburgh Festival of the Arts has its first season: the annual summer event will attract performers to Scotland from all over the globe.

1954 Quebec City's first Winter Carnival, organized by local businessmen, includes street dances, costume balls, ice-sculpture championships, a canoe race, speed skating, barrel-jumping, and skiing contests.

1930~1965

First Design Your Road

Interstates and postwar cars

It all points in one direction: 1959 Cadillac Sedan Deville.

In terms of scale, the largest things designed on this planet are probably cities, and the most numerous are the cars that move on the roads within them. One of the few admirable legacies of fascism is the superhighway. Italy already had a total of 550 km (340 miles) of autostrada when the first German inter-urban Autobahn, from Bonn to Cologne, was opened in 1932. The Autobahn was one of the symbols that let the world know that the National Socialists meant business. Unfortunately, as became apparent in 1939, it wasn't just for civilian transportation convenience.

The U.S. was impressed, and *Norman Bel Geddes's* (1893–1958) exhibit in the General Motors pavilion at the New York World's Fair of 1939 had shown the public what the future held for drivers. Streamlined cars would travel at 105 miles an hour on 14-lane superhighways lit by fluorescent strips in the curb. The post-WWII interstate expressway road-building project was influenced by these concepts, and the American public soon became familiar with the cloverleaf interchange.

GET YOUR KICKS ON ROUTE 66

The car barons who had done very well out of mechanizing American forces in World War II didn't have to try very hard to get the American public to buy a new auto. While in war-worn Europe there was a three-year waiting list for a new car, in the U.S. you could acquire a 1950 Cadillac Deville V8, with its 126-inch wheelbase, for $3,654—in pink.

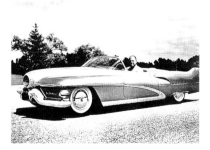

Harley Earl at the wheel of his 1954 Buick Le Sabre.

1955 The Citroën DS-19, introduced at the Automobile Show in Paris, is the first new model in two decades.

1961 The Weight-Watchers organization is founded in the U.S., by 214-pound Jean Nidetch.

1962 *West Side Story*, a musical updating of *Romeo and Juliet*, wins ten Oscars.

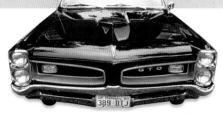

In your face: 1965 V8 Pontiac GTO, designed by John Z. DeLorean.

By 1969 there was one car per 2.4 people in the U.S. From 1927, when he joined General Motors, the king of style was *Harley Earl* (1893–1969), who had made his name in Hollywood designing "specials." While other companies had teams of designers, Earl singlehandedly stimulated the demand for cars by introducing annual model changes, even if they were cosmetic. He persuaded the engineers to press sheet steel into shapes never seen before. The soft curves of his designs were derived from the clay modeling technique he pioneered. In 1948 Cadillac made the first car with tailfins, a style that reached its peak with the 1959 Cadillac Eldorado Biarritz. The names are enough to make you want one!

ROUND, ROUND, GET AROUND...

While gas at only a few cents a gallon encouraged the V8 gas guzzler, Europe was the home of the sports car, and in the 1950s the postwar generation wanted a more stylish runabout. One of the first to borrow a European look had been the neat 1950 Studebaker Commander by

Raymond Loewy and colleagues, with its chrome circular grille. The first American sports car was General Motors's 1953 Chevrolet Corvette, the first production car to have a fiberglass body. Initially available only in white with a red vinyl interior, it was an instant cult object. In 1954 Ford's design team of Walker, Maguire, and Engel answered with the stylish Thunderbird, immortalized in the Beach Boys' line "...fun, fun, fun till her daddy took the T-Bird away." A perfect ending.

Bubble car

In 1956 Heinkel in Germany gave the world the 198cc Kabinenroller bubble car, to be followed by the Messerschmitt Tiger in 1958. But it wasn't all gloom in Europe—you could also buy a Porsche, if you had the cash.

Getting sporty: a tastily colored convertible Corvette.

1950 The first Japanese tape recorder, produced by Tokyo Tsushin Kogyo (Sony), weighs nearly 40 pounds, uses tape made from rice paper, and sells for around $500.

1961 Luciano Pavarotti makes his debut as Rodolfo in Puccini's *La Bohème* at the Teatro Municipale in Reggio Emilia.

1974 "Streaking" becomes a popular fad on both sides of the Atlantic, as males and females alike make naked dashes at college and public events.

1945~2000

Design by Digestion
Fast food

A place for everything… McDonald's is the acme of food packaging.

Look at all those burgers: same shape, same size. And the amazingly symmetrical pineapple rings. The massed ranks of bottles and cans. The armies of lookalike cola. It's all too much. There's no doubt that food and design go hand in hand, but is there a limit to what visuals can persuade you to buy? Do you care any more?

Since the 1940s, food packaging and graphic design have been important parts of daily life. Multinational food manufacturers battle in burger bars and supermarket aisles for our custom. They're designing food so we buy it and make them rich. Perhaps we ought to be worried.

Cool, cool water
Designer water. The phrase used to be a joke. Wasn't tap water good enough for the hippest board meetings? Evidently not: you've only to see the flood of bottled water products aping Perrier, during and since the 1980s, to understand a little of market forces. The ergonomic bottles commissioned by Vittel from the Japanese designer Matsayuki Kurokawa and from the Italian Gaetano Pesce, and that by Philippe Starck for Glacier are just (pardon me) a drop in the ocean.

A QUICK ONE
Fast food isn't new. *John* MONTAGUE, fourth Earl of Sandwich (1718–92), was a corrupt politician with a bad gambling habit, who wanted to be able to eat without leaving the gaming table. Need one say more? It was a great idea, and although the look and taste of a sandwich will be different wherever we come from, the concept's pretty much the same.

From there it's a short hop to the hamburger, a nineteenth-century German meat patty (you'd never have guessed?) taken to the U.S. and reintroduced to Europe a century later. Le Big Mac and Der Wimpey. *Sacre Bleu! Achtung!* And while we're eating on the run, don't let's forget good old British fish and chips. Whatever you think of these culinary delights, they're all presented cooked, packaged in boxes of cardboard or Styrofoam, or wrapped in newsprint, for near-instant consumption. Or in the case of a sandwich, sealed by an invisible hand into a see-through container you can wrestle with, and stamped with a sell-by date. Selling packaged food takes a little longer.

1980 "Scarsdale Diet" creator Dr. Herman Tarnower is shot fatally by headmistress Jean Struven Harris, who claims it was an accident.

1986 Superconductivity hits the headlines as Swiss physicist K .Alex Müller and German physicist J. Georg Bednorz of IBM's Zurich Research Laboratory discover zero resistance in a ceramic material that permits superconductivity at -397° F.

1997 Britain is badly hit by outbreaks of BSE; many countries ban imports of beef and beef products from Britain.

EVERY HOME SHOULD HAVE ONE

Hot stuff

A nice 1970s Breville sandwich toaster. Burn your tongue the easy way, and have enormous fun trying to clean off the cheese afterward.

DO YOUR OWN THING

Why do you buy this soup but not that one? Those chocolates but not these? Do you make your choice because of the taste, or because of the look of a product? Or both? Do you prefer plastic to glass? New or familiar shapes or labels? Think Heinz ketchup, Coca-Cola, Jiff peanut butter, Campbell's soup, Kellogg's cornflakes: it's a safe bet that at some point during your weekly zoom around the supermarket, you're buying into a series of design concepts. Are you really what you eat? Do you buy one to get one free? You might if it looked right. But why? Think about it.

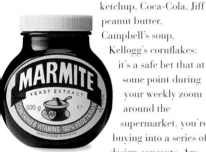

A popular English design classic.

HEY! PACK THAT UP!

Packaging is a world of its own, and it's amazing that something intentionally disposable is often far too good to throw away. The Japanese compartmentalized lunchbox is one such object, with a space for each specially wrapped course. At the other end of the scale, look at (or away from) the same process used by every airline caterer in the world. Late 1990s wine bottles have suddenly changed to new, chic shapes, cartons for every kind of drink show awareness of stowage and use, and supermarkets have designed their own labels for decades. It's certainly made eating and drinking a lot more interesting.

Wilmaaaaa!

As *The Flintstones* titles roll again, and Fred's car tips up under that Brontosaurus steak, reflect, gentle reader, on the crisis affecting some burger chains. By the late 1980s, marketing had guaranteed that the Big M owned over 9,000 outlets worldwide, and served nearly 100,000 customers every minute. Ten years on, with genetically modified foods under suspicion, and Styrofoam containers held at more than arm's length because of their effect on global warming, things aren't quite so straightforward.

The shape of the bottle is what makes you pick it up.

1941 Japanese schoolchildren collect a million tons of acorns to help ease severe food shortages.

1950 Americans "Relax and Mambo" to the latest dance craze, introduced from Cuba.

1955 The London Clean Air Act bans the burning of untreated coal to prevent a recurrence of the smog of 1952 and to save an estimated £90 million per year spent repairing corrosion damage and cleaning up the soot.

1930~1965

Relax, It's Only Wood
Plywood furniture

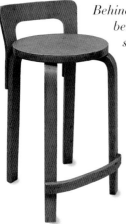

Behind every great man...Well, behind the male movers and shakers of twentieth-century design, there are many good women. Charles Eames's wife Ray and Alvar Aalto's wife Aino are just two: great partners, overshadowed by their men.

Husband and wife team: Ray and Charles Eames.

Alvar Aalto's solid wood stacking stool, designed in 1932 for Korhonen.

Alvar AALTO (1898–1976) was a main-man of Finnish design, a "great" in Europe and, above all, a real king of plywood, someone who could make the stuff into sensitive and useful shapes. Aino advised—but seriously. The Aaltos respected improvements in materials and advances in technology, as long as comfort came out on top. Their designs—stools, trolleys, and tables—are still made today. Most experts reckon that the pinnacle of Alvar's achievement was the Paimio Sanatorium (1929–33): a "total" concept, and a chair to go with it—a one-piece plywood form with molded seat and back that went mass-produced in 1935. Plus the Stacking Stool No. 60: yes—you know it well.

Boring boring plywood
You want the basic facts? This stuff is so common, but really strong. Layers (you decide how many) of thin sheets of wood (called plies) are laid and glued so the grain of one sheet is at a ninety-degree angle to the next, and so on, alternately. It gives the stuff strength every which way.

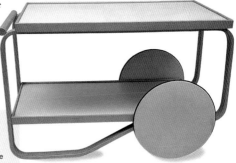

Not quite a wheelbarrow, but the same principle: a tea trolley in bent laminated wood by Alvar Aalto (1936).

1960 The 15,000-ton hospital ship *Hope* leaves San Francisco on September 22, bound for Indonesia.

1963 Valium (diazepam) is launched in the U.S. by Roche Laboratories.

1965 Edgard Varèse, a pioneer of electronic music, dies. His 1958 *Poème électronique* was broadcast on 425 speakers at the Brussels World Fair.

CHARLES EAMES

Please put your hands together for King Charles: Plywood King, that is, of the U.S.A. *Charles EAMES* (1907–78) takes up hyperspace in the textbooks. As a young design guru (he was head of the Cranbrook Academy of Art, Michigan, 1937–40),

Charles Eames's hugely successful lounge chair and ottoman, 1956.

Eames pushed plywood as a medium from the 1940s, with a process called "cycle-welding," used on objects made entirely from wood.

His best-known designs—lounge and dining chairs, home storage units (OK, cupboards)—spread all over the globe. The apex was the Eames Lounge Chair and Ottoman (1956), made of pressed rosewood shells and a cast aluminum base, and mass produced by Herman Miller. A classic, imitated now in your local furniture warehouse.

Eames was as good in plastics and metal as he was with plywood, and at Pacific Palisades he designed a house with Mrs. E that was a model for the later Modern movement in design.

DESIGNER NAMES

The Dane **Arne Jacobsen** *(1902–71) was another who was bitten by the plywood bug, but was also a fine designer of tableware. He spent World War II in Sweden making wallpaper, and diversified afterward, with wood as a main theme. Jacobsen's most famous moment was with a three-legged stacking chair, a lovely affair with a plywood back and three tubular-steel legs. He didn't stop there. Leaving wood to the trees, Jacobsen's Swan and Egg chairs progressed with fiberglass shells, aluminum legs, and padding. They were great, but there's nothing like the real thing.*

DESIGNER NAMES

No plywood here: Arne Jacobsen's Egg chair, made of fiberglass, 1958.

1956 The first Eurovision song contest takes place in Lugano and is won by the Swiss entrant Lyss Alyssia.

1961 New York's Metropolitan Museum pays $350,000 for Rembrandt's painting *Aristotle Contemplating the Bust of Homer*, the highest auction price ever paid so far for a work of art.

1965 Danish brewers Carlsberg and Tuborg have a strike, causing a national beer shortage.

1950~1975

You Are What You Look Like
Graphic design

"Graphic design" is a profession invented in the 1950s in the United States. Before that, there were typographers, commercial artists, and jobbing printers. Most companies had muddled along on their nineteenth-century house styles or turned to the local printer or advertising agent for their image. For half a century, Europe had led all the design trends, but now, as with so many other things, it was America's turn. American business realized that you had to look good to your public.

Magazines led the way. Distinguished titles, most founded in the late nineteenth century, competed with one another for the best designers, photographers, and illustrators. Titles like *The Saturday Evening Post, Harper's Bazaar, Colliers', Fortune*, and *Time* vied with each other on the newsstand.

The U.S. benefited from émigré designers who had fled from Germany, like *Herbert BAYER* (1900–85) and *Herbert MATTER*

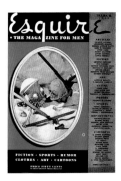

Neat, effective graphic design: *Esquire* in March 1938.

(1907–84), who brought the latest design ideas from Europe. *Paul RAND* (1914–96) embraced them and refined them to reflect

Sentimentality in 1926, consumerism in 1933: magazine covers acting as mirrors to society.

U.S. needs with stylish cover designs for *Direction* in the 40s. His 1956 corporate identity for IBM brought the idea of branding dramatically up to date. *Henry WOLF* (b. 1925) created the stylish look of *Esquire* and *Harper's Bazaar*, and *Lester BEALL* (1903–69) did more than any other designer to turn packaging from a ragbag of odds and ends to a unified look. The rise of the supermarket accelerated the need for packaging to shout from the shelf, and many traditional designs were updated.

1966 In Italy, heavy rain causes the River Arno to burst its banks, causing severe floods to Florence, damaging or destroying many of the city's art treasures.

1973 Actor Marlon Brando refuses an Oscar in protest against Hollywood's exploitation of Native Americans.

1974 Hawaiian pineapples account for only 33 percent of the world crop, down from 72 percent in 1950.

SON OF BAUHAUS

While America modernized its graphic design style, Switzerland in the mid-50s showed there was more ticking than clocks. The sort of rational, ordered thinking and visual precision that helped make watches produced the "Swiss International Style." A key figure in its development was painter, sculptor, and architect-designer *Max BILL* (1908–88), who encouraged a combination of Bauhaus principles (he was an ex-student) and Constructivism at the Ulm Hochschule für Gestaltung, where he was director from 1951. Founded in 1950, the school was a memorial to Hans and Sophie Scholl, who had been executed by the Nazis, and involved itself in product design, architecture, and graphic design through teamwork. The Ulm school perfected a very logical, pared-down sort of design.

Originating in Zurich and Basel, and guided by *Josef MÜLLER-BROCKMAN* (b.1914) and *Armin HOFMANN* (b.1920), respectively, the Swiss graphic style has become one of clearest descriptions of functional communication—the exact opposite of the emotional exotic designs that were to follow. Its characteristics? Clear, simple images, usually photographs, sans serif types, and simple, undecorated composition. It typified a clean and unglamorous style that was the undisputed design look well into the 1970s.

DESIGNER NAMES

Some designs are instantly recognizable, but the names behind them are often less so. **Gerald Holtom***? The English designer in 1961 of what was to become one of the best-known non-commercial symbols in the world, the "Ban the Bomb" logo for CND (Campaign for Nuclear Disarmament). Likewise, Nike's world famous "swoosh" logo was designed in 1971 for the new company by a graphic design student,* **Carolyn Davidson***, for a fee of $35.*

Attractive. Reliable. Economical.
The new VW 1600s.
Bigger and better value for money.

only 1

first direct

Purity in print

Typefaces usually reflect the age and culture in which they are designed. If Swiss design deserved a typeface, it was Helvetica, designed in 1958 by Max Miedinger and Edouard Hoffman.

Typical Helvetica clarity. Attractive, reliable, direct…

1932 Motorized hand-cranked "stabiles" by American sculptor-painter Alexander Calder excite public and critics alike in Paris.

1944 General MacArthur drops a million Christmas cards over the Philippines from the air.

1957 Three U.S. Air Force jets complete a nonstop round-the-world flight averaging more than 500 miles an hour.

1920~1980

Turn On, Tune In
Radio

A nice night in by the radio.

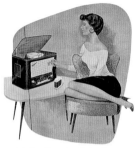

Modern living in 1955: style and leisure from a German radio advertisement.

Some products have stayed virtually the same since they were first designed—the upright Hoover vacuum, for instance, and the refrigerator. The radio, by virtue of being a collection of components in a box, has been able to adapt its shape to prevailing trends. The earliest tube receivers of the 1920s were designed by engineers and put in sturdy wooden cases that doubled as furniture. As radio caught on, case designs became more adventurous, and the popular sets of the 30s reflected the architectural tastes of the period—the fretwork sunrise in the speaker grille being a desirable symbol of modernity.

Bakelite, patented in 1907 (*see page 81*) liberated radio design: it was an ideal material with excellent electrical qualities, robust, and wood-colored. The British Ekco company, which had invested heavily in Bakelite molding machinery, created the radical radio, the Ekco AD65, designed by Canadian architect *Wells Coates* (1895–1958). He adopted modernist simplicity, opting for a round radio with a semicircular dial surrounding the speaker.

As the economies of Western Europe, Japan, and the U.S. slowly began to pick themselves up after World War II, new

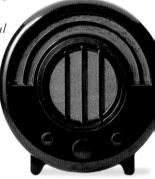

Wells Coates's simple and elegant design for the front of the Ekco AD65.

ideas were needed for new products to go into new homes. The war period had been one of domestic deprivation, and now the more adventurous manufacturers turned to fresh design ideas—often stimulated (surprise, surprise) by technical advances that the war effort had accelerated.

1961 The student revue "Beyond the Fringe" debuts in London's West End to packed houses, launching the careers of Alan Bennett, Peter Cook, Dudley Moore, and Jonathan Miller.

1974 The "Heimlich maneuver," described in the June issue of *Emergency Medicine* by Cincinnati surgeon Henry Jay Heimlich, will save thousands of people from choking to death on food.

1978 The Magimix food processor revolutionizes home cooking all over the world.

Walk, don't run!

The invention of the transistor and the microchip have transformed the products around us, particularly in size. Personal, portable entertainment was conceived by Sony's chairman Akio Morita while playing golf in the mid-70s, because he wanted to be able to listen to his favorite music in stereo while outdoors. Critics thought it would be a flop—how wrong can you be?

Life changed—again—when tubes gave way to transistors and radios became easily portable.

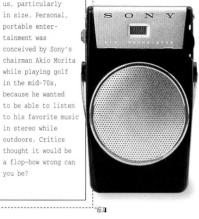

graduates of the Ulm School of Design *(see page 97)*. Between them they showed the success a company could have if it put design first. Clean lines and attention to detail became Braun's trademark, and they rapidly became a household name, with toasters, mixers, razors, hairdryers, and radios.

One of Braun's most famous designs, which challenged the look of postwar record players, was the Phonosuper (1956). A rectangular case of white plastic and pale wood with a Plexiglas lid, it is affectionately known as "Snow White's Coffin."

BRAUN BOX

When two brothers, Artur and Erwin Braun, inherited their father's small electrical company in 1951, they hired top designers including *Dieter RAMS* (b.1932) and *Hans GUGELOT* (1920–65), both

Gugelot and Rams's pioneering combined radio and record player of 1956, the Phonosuper.

You will hear this

The Nazi propaganda ministry realized the importance of its citizens' hearing their message, and Hitler endorsed the production of the Volksempfanger—peoples' radio—which was subsidized by the state. Its neat, rectangular Bakelite case was based on an advanced 1926 design by Walter Kersting—who, ironically, was opposed to the Nazi regime. Conveniently for the Nazis, it was not able to receive overseas broadcasts.

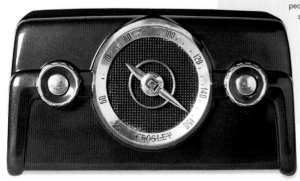

An American radio from 1950, with styling noticeably similar to a car dashboard.

1950 Charles Schulz's comic strip "Peanuts" debuts in the U.S., under its original title "Li'l Folks."

1953 American physician Henry Swan II lowers body temperature to slow circulation and permit dry-heart surgery, or "cryosurgery."

1961 Bob Dylan, age 21, plays his first gig at Gerde's Folk City, Greenwich Village, New York.

1950~1970

Movie Magic
Film credits and posters

Early Bass, edgy, unsettling, paranoid, in keeping with the movie's drug theme.

Postwar movies gave the U.S. and Britain some of their lasting "highs," and even now it's hard to beat the impact made in the 1950s and 60s by Saul BASS (1920–96), first in the U.S. and soon after in Britain. He's been called the inventor of the modern film title, and it's hard to disagree. Based on Sunset Boulevard since the late 1940s, Bass (now Bass Yager Citigate) used a single, distinctive graphic concept or motif to create variations on a theme that, together, would form the basis for a film's opening titles, and all its advertising, from newspaper to billboard.

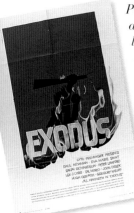

Bass again, this time reaching out for the promised land.

Check out some of his earliest designs: *The Man with the Golden Arm* (1955), *Anatomy of a Murder* (1959), and *Exodus* (1960), all simple, magnetic images. At a stroke they salute modern European art and design, especially Matisse and the great American typographer *Paul RAND* (1914–96). Bass extended his stylistic range in *West Side Story* (1961) and *Walk on the Wild Side* (1962), and his input from opening credits to whole sequences in *Psycho* (1960) and *Grand Prix* (1966). We've him to thank for the extended credit

EVERY HOME SHOULD HAVE ONE

Cut! and paste
…a classic film poster of some sort: no, not the stuff that falls out of magazines, but the real McCoy—something with an indelible link to the era it portrays. Bond. Bass. Binder—now that would be something. But keep it safe: it'll be a classic.

sequences we've become used to in film and TV. Early on, Bass seized the chance to utilize contemporary music, especially jazz or percussion rhythms, to create extra impact and to set a scene through simple animated forms.

1964 Finnish dockworker Toimi Solvo stays awake for 16 days and 10 hours, with the help of regular snow massages and strong coffee.

1965 The new Zeeland Bridge is the longest bridge in Europe, connecting North Beveland with Schouwen-Duiveland more than a mile away and reducing the 90-mile Rotterdam–Flushing journey by 20 miles.

1970 Mae West makes a short-lived movie comeback after 27 years, playing alongside Raquel Welch in Gore Vidal's sex-change movie *Myra Breckinridge*.

DESIGNER NAMES

For an offbeat balance between Bass and Rand, search out the c. 300 posters by Cologne-born theater-designer **Peter Strausfeld** *(1910–80, a.k.a. Peter Pendrey), advertising the programs at London's Academy Cinema, 1948–80. Instantly recognizable, these were big, superb expressionist woodcut prints, strong in modern wood-block typography. They are unique individually and as a series in the history of world cinema advertising. Each was an instant statement about a film, its subject, and the Academy's philosophy.*

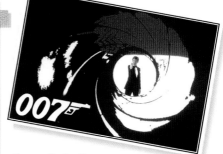

The compelling Bond intro sequence brings you face to face with the coolest, meanest, and most dangerous man in the British Secret Service.

REALLY, DOUBLE-O-SEVEN!

Elsewhere, others were working along very similar lines. Ian Fleming's creation James Bond stepped onto celluloid in *Dr. No* (1964), accompanied by a film credit by *Maurice BINDER* (d. 1991) and a riveting musical theme by John Barry. Binder's credits were a sensational combination of motion, freeze-frame, blood-red filters, a camera lens, and bullet holes, stark and dark: nothing like them had been seen before in British cinema.

More than 35 years later, Binder's credits and Barry's music remain an item: they've stayed with Bond, with variations. And you still get to see major action before the main credits roll.

COMIC CREDITS

Comedy especially profited from graphic designers rising to the challenge of film credits. Peter Sellers's Pink Panther films. *Those Magnificent Men in Their Flying Machines* (1965), with its superb credits by Ronald Searle. And finally Disney awoke: one of its best, and unsung, credits was for *Bedknobs and Broomsticks* (1971), a parody of the Norman Bayeux Tapestry, with ideas that just keep on going.

The Pink Panther: French chic mixed with a certain *je ne sais comment*.

PETER SELLERS
in
THE
PINK
PANTHER
STRIKES
AGAIN
BLAKE EDWARDS'

THE ALL-NEW ADVENTURES OF THE WORLD'S MOST BUMBLING DETECTIVE

1962 Decca Records turns downs the Beatles and signs Brian Poole and the Tremeloes instead.

1967 U.S. and British pantyhose sales climb as women take to the miniskirt.

1967 Albania declares itself the world's first officially atheist state.

1960~1970

Please Please Me

Sixties culture

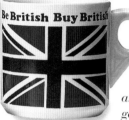

Decades are artificial markers, but things did change dramatically between the 1950s and 60s. Underlying design and lifestyle was social change. At a time of full employment, a new generation had new money to spend. A mood of regeneration, youth, and possibility dawned. This was the age that gave birth to street style, and the word "design" began to be used in everyday conversation.

A Union Jack mug showed your Pop patriotism.

Everything seemed to make a quantum leap—fashion, magazines, art, hairstyles, TV, cars. It was an exciting time, when it seemed easy to open a boutique, or become a photographer or an interior designer. In Britain, London's Carnaby Street became a mecca of the new trendy youth fashion market, eager for sharp suits (very un-Savile Row, only two blocks away), floppy vinyl caps, Union Jack trays and towels.

GREAT EMPIRES ARE FROM A DISHTOWEL BORN

Several big fashion names became established in the sixties. One was *Laura Ashley* (1926–88), who started her empire by printing her dishtowel designs on her kitchen table. A young entrepreneur-designer named *Terence Conran* (b.1931)

Car of the decade?

No, not the Mini, the Jaguar E-type. Designed by Malcolm Sayer, an aerodynamicist, using mathematical formulae to produce its stunning shape, and anticipating the use of CAD (computer-aided design) by decades. He created one of the most desirable cars ever designed.

The Mini? OK, it was technically innovative and has a cult following, but pretty? No.

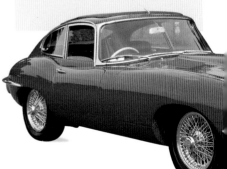

1966 Barclaycard, the first British credit card, is introduced.

1967 Aretha Franklin has four top-ten hits in the U.S., three of them selling over a million copies each.

1969 President Nixon bans production of chemical and biological warfare agents.

EVERY HOME SHOULD HAVE ONE

Every home has probably had one

Owen Maclaren was an ex-aero-engineer, who in 1967 devised one of the most useful designs for the young mother. Inspired by the way aircraft wheels folded, he created the baby stroller, since much imitated and improved upon.

POSTER, POSTER ON THE WALL...

The poster had been the major advertising medium before the arrival of TV. Now it had a new life on the bedroom and living room wall. A sheet of paper printed with the right design could confirm your credibility, so a Che Guevara poster, or a girl with no panties scratching her behind at a tennis net, could make or break you.

The kings of poster art in Britain were *Michael ENGLISH* and *Roger DEAN* (both b. 1940). Michael English was a pioneer of the British version of psychedelia; on the West Coast his equivalents were *Wes WILSON* (b.1937) and *Victor MOSCOSO* (b.1936). Roger Dean was a graduate in three-dimensional design who used his very popular graphic images for rock groups such as Yes as a platform to try out his ideas for fantastic and extravagant architecture.

opened his first shop, Habitat, in Fulham in 1964, and revolutionized the way you could furnish your house or apartment. Half a mile away in Chelsea, *Mary QUANT* (b. 1934) opened her first Bazaar boutique.

And the music—what is music but designed sound? The sixties resonated to the talent of a new fresh youth culture, from a class of people who had traditionally been denied expression. Staid fine art was rocked by upstart working-class artists (almost a contradiction in terms till then). The pop artist *Peter BLAKE* (b.1932) designed the cover for the Beatles' *Sgt Pepper's Lonely Hearts Club Band* with help from his wife, sculptor Jann Howarth.

Che Guevara, favorite icon of the armchair revolutionary.

Fold it

Many a designer-inventor has been thwarted by having their ideas rejected by established manufacturers. Auto engineer Alex Moulton (b.1920) (he had designed the suspension for the Mini—the car, not the skirt) wasn't the first person to think of a small-wheeled bike, ideal for the housewife shopper (who never used it!), but his 1960 minibike design had rubber suspension and could be folded to go in the back of a car. He was turned down by the cycle industry and had to set up manufacturing on his own. A few years later, they sheepishly bought him out.

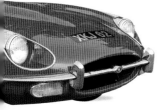

The most beautiful car in the world? The E-type, a designer's wet dream.

DESIGN ~ A CRASH COURSE **103**

1961 Trans World Airlines introduces in-flight movies, showing *By Love Possessed* on its New York to San Francisco route.

1967 Japanese microwave oven production soars as many Japanese households change directly from hibachi grills to microwave ovens.

1978 *Space Invaders*, the first arcade video game, causes a sensation worldwide.

1950~2000
Rising Suns
Japan makes good

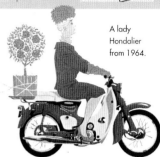

A lady Hondalier from 1964.

The distant sound of Hondas in the hills wasn't a figment of anyone's imagination. Nor were sales of five million Honda Super Cub motorbikes between 1958 and 1967. The Japanese had arrived. A synthesis of late-twentieth-century Japanese design might be a Shinto figure astride a classy motorbike, Walkman clipped to belt, filming the effect with a camcorder resembling a prosthetic limb. Bizarre?

Postwar competition from Japanese industry was either feared or pooh-poohed in the prejudiced West—mostly pooh-poohed—but from 1950 to 1980 the Japanese rethought their own ideas on design and manufacture in order to become competitive again in worldwide trade. In the 1950s, several of the biggest Japanese industrialists—including the heads of Hitachi, Matsushita, and Honda—went fact-finding. Stateside, scrutinizing corporate design and industrial practice.

Result: by 1980 many Japanese consumer goods surpassed Western products in quality and price. OK, so some companies used Italian designers in the 1970s. But check your own belongings. Your vacuum cleaner. Your stereo. VCR. TV. Washing machine. Microwave. Wristwatch. Even your car is quite possibly Japanese, at least in design.

Older than you think...
Hard to imagine that the Toyoda (later Toyota) company was established in 1898, isn't it? Just think: if Toyoda had known about Ambrose Heal's first furniture catalog of the same year, the world might have been an extraordinary place!

Toyota Yaris, the Japanese Clio.

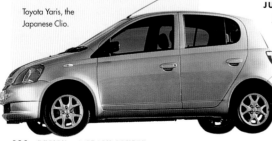

JUST FOR YOU
Japanese design succeeded because Japanese designers were sensitive enough to make products that appealed to at least three of our five demanding senses: looking good, sounding

1983 Tokyo's Metropolitan Teien Art Museum opens in a renovated 1932 Art Deco mansion.

1989 U.S. aircraft *Voyager 2* sends back pictures of the planet Neptune and Triton, one of its moons.

1993 Japan has her worst rice harvest for decades and imports foreign rice to make up for the shortfall.

good, feeling good. Since the 1950s Sony—like many other Japanese enterprises—had run its own design department. In 1978, after a lot of research and development by in-house design groups. Sony finally brought all of these sense appeals together in the Walkman.

By that time Japanese design had worked hard to establish itself across a wide field, sometimes a bit hit or miss, but always busy, always trying something new: clock radios, anodized aluminum effects for cassette players. Switches, knobs, tactile stuff to keep youth happy. Testing ergonomic ideas: after all, you have to be able to hold your Nikon in comfort. But now you can play with your PlayStation in an emotionally rewarding way: no self-inflicted wounds.

And Japanese graphic design kept pace, initially using European Constructivist ideas and then—during the 1960s—regaining its own self-esteem, urged on by influential American designers (especially Raymond Loewy). One result was the series of pictograms developed for the 1964 Tokyo Olympics. Their influence on Western design in this area was a real indication of the way things were going.

Can you feel it?

Hard to imagine that the grip of your camcorder has been influenced by Japanese philosophy? Try harder. The Shinto idea that the most inanimate objects have their own spirit has outlets in design technology. If it didn't feel good, you wouldn't use it. Or wear it. Or carry it. The overall need to achieve something close to perfection has a place in Japanese design, whatever the object, however hi-tech. Just because you find it so easy to carry, it may have eluded you that the concept of your camcorder is that it is indeed a logical extension of your body.

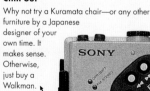

EVERY HOME SHOULD HAVE ONE

Chill out

Why not try a Kuramata chair—or any other furniture by a Japanese designer of your own time. It makes sense. Otherwise, just buy a Walkman.

SONY

Sony's Walkman, probably Japan's greatest hit.

1960 Soviet leader Nikita Khrushchev rudely bangs his shoe on his desk during a speech to the United Nations General Assembly by Philippine delegate Lorenzo Sumulong.

1978 Unemployment figures rise throughout the world, with a U.S. rate of 6 percent, Britain 6.1 percent, France 5.5, and West Germany 3.4 percent.

1980 New York's 30-story hotel, the Grand Hyatt, opens its doors. It has a mirrored glass façade, an atrium four stories high, and 1,400 rooms.

1960~2000

Are You Sitting Comfortably?
Chairs

To chart the history of design, this book could have been entirely devoted to the chair. Materials, techniques, changing fashions…They may have an obvious basic function, but as with so many other possessions, we sometimes want to stand back and admire them.

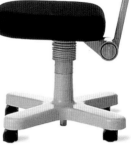

Brightening the office is the Sedia Dattilo by Sottsass, Jr., taking a leaf out of the old man's book.

Things changed in the 1960s when the tradition of buying sound, reliable furniture made to last gave way to style considerations, and as traditional methods gave way to mass-production techniques. New materials, particularly plastic, liberated the design possibilities.

ITALIANS HAVE MORE FUN

In serious, creative, experimental furniture design, the Italians have shown the way. Companies like Artemide, Cassina, Zanotta, and Kartell have long reaped the benefits of employing the most inventive and original minds. In the 60s and 70s, Italian designers were quick to explore the style possibilities of new plastics, as in the design by *Joe COLOMBO* (1930–71) for the first all-plastic stacking chair, the Universale for Kartell (1965). In 1969 *Vico MAGISTRETTI* (b.1920) made his elegant Selene chair for Artemide in bright-colored glossy fiberglass.

New stretch fabrics made fantastic sculptural sofas and easy chairs possible, a chance not missed by the "Memphis" designers. Drawn together in Italy in the 1980s by *Ettore SOTTSASS* (b.1917),

1985 A hole in the ozone layer is discovered over Antarctica; many blame it on CFCs (chlorofluorocarbons), while others claim it is just a seasonal disturbance.

1993 The World Health Organization declares that tuberculosis threatens to kill 30 million people in the next 10 years and could become incurable if efforts are not increased to control the disease.

1999 90,000 people watch the American women's soccer team beat China on penalties to win the Women's World Cup.

Memphis excelled in the celebration of borrowed decorative styles that redefined the visual possibilities. The American *Peter SHIRE*'s (b.1947) jokey Bel Air asymmetric armchair in 1982, and Sottsass's own 1983 Westside collection of primary-colored easy chairs for the American company Knoll showed how quickly the mainstream had accepted their visual revolution.

Gehry's cardboard Little Beaver: ecological awareness with post-modern irreverence.

WHAT'S IN A NAME?

The 1980s allowed for eccentricity and an even more varied range of experimentation as the chair became an art object. *Frank O. GEHRY* (b.1929), architect of the Bilbao Guggenheim Museum, let his hair down with an armchair of corrugated cardboard called Little Beaver in 1980. *Philippe STARCK* (b.1949) had already made his name as the enfant terrible of design, and had three strikingly different chairs to his name when Kartell launched his highly successful "Dr. Glob" in 1988, dramatically contrasting steel back with red plastic seat and legs. More recently, Starck has refined

the subtleties of plastic forms further with his "Dr. No" and "Miss Trip" chairs.

These names reflect postmodernism's irreverence, and humor is evident in *Danny LANE*'s (b.1955) Etruscan glass chair of 1984: a chair you would be nervous about sitting in. Lighthearted designs by *Gaetano PESCE* (b.1939) include a portable chair that folds up like an umbrella, and his 1993 Broadway chair that looks as if it has escaped from a comic strip: spindly metal legs with springs on the feet, and a seat and back that appear to be made from hard candy.

In 1938 *Hans CORAY* (b.1906) designed the Landi, a modest chair made entirely of aluminum with a stamped perforated seat. It was light and stackable, could be used outdoors, is still in production fifty years later, and now attracts many imitators. In England it inspired *Rodney KINSMAN* (b.1943), who made his name with his 1971 Omstak steel chair.

The Etruscan chair: do you sit on it or stand around admiring it?

107

1869 The Harvard Medical School rejects a demand by President Charles W. Eliot that students be given written examinations, as most of the students cannot write well enough.

1941 Danish-born sculptor Gutzon Borglum dies just before completing his vast cliffside carvings of Presidents Thomas Jefferson, George Washington, Abraham Lincoln, and Theodore Roosevelt at Mount Rushmore.

1956 Rock paintings dating from 3500 B.C. and found 900 miles from Algiers establish that the Sahara must once have been fertile land.

1850~1985

Squelch
Organic inspiration—and antithesis

Nature's designs don't always transfer to the human realm...

Walking on a beach, you pick up a shell and admire its natural beauty—people have been doing this for thousands of years. There is a human inclination to find natural forms attractive; their design has been honed by need over millions of years. Natural forms have often been an inspiration to the designer. James Paxton was famously inspired by the giant lily pad to create the cast-iron framework for the Crystal Palace in 1850. In 1920s revolutionary Russia Petr MITURICH (1887–1956) designed (but never built) some bizarre vehicles based on animal locomotion. Could Leonardo's tank have been inspired by a tortoise shell?

You could say that there was an organic quality about much of the streamlining style of the 1930s; obviously, after 200 million years of evolution, a shark will end up streamlined. Think how fishlike the earliest submarine designs were. They worked. In contrast, early airplane designers were rather bird-obsessed, but flapping wings are not easy to mechanize. When applied to design, this natural influence is called biomorphism.

POSTWAR SMOOTH
The swooping curves of the postwar sports car, like *Ben BOWDEN*'s (1906–98) 1946 design for the Healey 2.4-liter sedan, and *William LYONS*'s (1901–85) XK120 Jaguar in 1948, had pleasant, "natural" contours.

Film effect
Films have frequently influenced design, and the most organic of designs was the unpleasant world that illustrator H. R. Geiger created for Ridley Scott's *Alien*. We can see an influence of his esthetic in some of the more adventurous portable CD players of recent years, and in one of Colani's designs that was realized, the curvaceous black CB10 camera for Canon in 1983. The helmets worn by the Star Troopers in *Star Wars* (1978) quickly influenced the full-face motorcycle helmet.

The smooth lines of Bowden's 1946 bicycle reflected the influence of natural forms.

Bowden's most organic design, though, was his futuristic bicycle, which caused a sensation at the 1946 "Britain can make it" exhibition.

The IBM Selectric cries out to be touched, which must have been encouraging for 60s secretaries.

The soft lines of the IBM Selectric golf-ball typewriter, designed in 1961 by *Elliot Noyes* (1910–77), a major figure in American industrial design, were derived from his use of sculptural modeling, and give it a "please touch me" quality not common in mass-produced objects.

The master of organic design is Italian-Swiss *Luigi Colani* (b.1928), who abhors straight lines. Like Norman Bel Geddes before him, he has designed a stream of futuristic vehicles: liners, cars, trucks, planes, but also shotguns and crossbows. All feature soft, flowing forms that reject the dull "black box" look that predominated in the late 70s. Perhaps the most obvious and appropriate biomorphic design is the beautiful spiraling Nautilus speaker designed by Kenneth Grange of Pentagram in 1976 and manufactured by B&W.

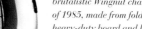

1958 Acupuncture is used for the first time as an anesthetic after nearly 5,000 years of use in medical therapy in China.

1962 American company Dow Corporation of Michigan invents silicone breast implants.

1974 British beauty queen Helen Morgan resigns as Miss World when it is discovered that she has an illegitimate child.

1955~1990

It's Everywhere
Plastic profusion

A cool Danish water heater, in polypropylene.

Plastic has come a long way since the solid reliability of Bakelite. By the 1970s designers could choose from a spectrum of plastics with a broad range of characteristics—and lots of names beginning with "poly."

The first conquest was the kitchen. Polyethylene ruled here in the form of the anonymous sink liner, and more importantly (in design terms), the Tupperware box, the brainchild of Earl Tupper in the 1950s. When polypropylene, tougher than polyethylene, arrived in the 60s it was strong enough for furniture design, and enabled *Robin DAY* (b.1915) to design the classic stackable chair for Hille.

If polyethylene was soft and pliable, another new plastic, melamine, was the first challenge to traditional ceramics by being tough and long-lasting—and it could be washed in one of those newfangled dishwashers. In Britain, plastics designer A. H. Woodfull took advantage of the strong color possibilities and the new shapes made possible by injection molding; his 1950s cruet set is now a collector's item.

Another type of plastic, vinyl, brought about a 60s icon, the inflatable armchair by Quasar Khahn. In the 80s the Memphis group in Italy managed to breathe life into the laminated surface by reworking 50s decorative surface designs and jazzing up the colors. By applying them to eccentric-shaped furniture, they created the most memorable style of the 80s.

One of many vinyl inflatable armchairs beloved of Italian designers in the 1960s.

1977 George Lucas's sci-fi adventure *Star Wars* becomes the biggest earner in movie history.

1987 More than 32,000 Americans have been diagnosed as suffering from AIDS and 60 percent of them have died.

1989 A Robert Mapplethorpe exhibition is canceled in New York because some of his homoerotic photographs are judged obscene.

PLASTIC RULES

Now practically every consumer product relies on a plastic component or case, and design is the factor that persuades you to buy one product rather than another. From the moment you arise and clean your teeth, possibly with a Goupil toothbrush designed by Philippe Starck, to the moment you set your alarm clock, your daily life depends on plastics, and it's up to designers to invest this useful material with likeable qualities. Around the house we have Rowenta irons, Braun razors, Philips radios, and just when we thought we had seen everything, frosted jelly plastic becomes the late 90s trend. While product reliability has greatly improved, enabling products to last longer, rapid technological change encourages us to spend money on the latest gadget: mobile phone, global positioning, minidisk, DVD player, digital camera, etc.

DECORATE YOURSELF WITH PLASTIC

Before plastic became tainted with the "cheap and nasty" reputation, it enjoyed great popularity as a material for costume jewelry. The transparency of plastic, and its scope for bright coloring, created a vogue in the 1920s and 30s for some marvelously gaudy jewelry.

EVERY HOME SHOULD HAVE ONE

Swatch

Once, you expected a watch to last a lifetime, but mass-production has revolutionized the useful gadget on your wrist. You can now afford several watches for different occasions. If you have been seduced by Swatch's clever marketing, you will even be collecting them.

Wise Hand, a Swatch design from 1996: have you got this in your collection?

After World War II came a new transparent plastic, trademarked as Lucite in the U.S. and Perspex in Britain, and claimed as "the gemstone of modern industry." A craft industry grew up in the late 40s recycling surplus aircraft canopies and carving them into brooches. In the 1960s Susan Fry, a student at London's Royal College of Art, had the idea of chunky rings made of multicolored sandwiched Lucite. They were inset with messages such as LOVE—very 60s—and have enjoyed several revivals since.

Plastic jewelry by Cicada, a craft group that exploited the decorative qualities of new resin materials.

1919 The pogo stick is invented and inspires a dance routine in the Ziegfeld Follies.

1947 A Bedouin boy exploring a cave at Qumran, northwest of Palestine's Dead Sea, discovers an earthenware jar containing scrolls of parchment that include all but two small parts of the Old Testament Book of Isaiah.

1973 The Dutch ban driving on Sundays in an attempt to preserve gasoline supplies, while other countries impose a 50mph speed limit.

1900~2000

Toy Story

Toys

There is a parallel universe. Sometimes we accidentally stray into it, and we used to spend a lot of time there. It's called Toyland. Toys aren't a new idea—there are beautiful examples in ancient tombs. In Europe, toy production has long been a traditional industry centered around Nuremberg, in Germany, where wooden toys date back to the Middle Ages. Nuremberg is still the location of the largest toy fair in the world.

New York, or Legolopolis, made from everyone's favorite building bricks.

Toys have always reflected the grown-up world, so when industrialization came along, so did the toy train and car, made in metal. The tin toy reigned supreme in the early twentieth century, with companies like Bing and Märklin manufacturing on a large scale. Gender roles were encouraged with dolls for girls and trains for boys.

Frank HORNBY (1863–1936) in England was inspired by a crane to make a miniature version of it, and the Meccano construction kit was born, founding a mighty toy empire and the inspiration for generations of engineers. In 1932 Meccano diversified into the die-cast Dinky toy line, now highly collectible miniature vehicles that swallowed many a schoolboy's allowance in the 1950s and 60s.

Pioneer
The first child's scooter was designed in 1897 by a 15-year-old boy, Walter Lines, but he didn't patent it, since his father, a toy manufacturer, didn't think it would catch on. He went on to found Lines Brothers and Triang Toys, which in 1964 took over the Hornby empire in Britain.

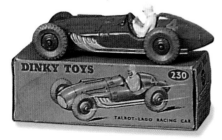

Dinky cars were the focus of every British boy's play world in the 1950s. If he had the prescience to keep them in good shape for his old age, so much the better.

1980 In Britain, Rubik's cube is voted "toy of the year."

1986 Nintendo video games debut in the U.S. and wow youngsters with sophisticated graphics.

1994 Former world heavyweight boxing champion George Foreman regains his title in Las Vegas, knocking out Michael Moorer in the tenth round to become the oldest boxer ever to win a title in any weight class.

PLASTIC PEOPLE

Some of the earliest (and highly flammable) plastic manufactured goods were celluloid dolls in the early 1900s. The first toys made with the much-improved plastics available after World War II were toy soldiers; barnyard animals followed soon after. Since then, wood and metal have given way to a tide of smooth, hygienic plastic.

Perhaps the best-known piece of plastic in the world is Barbie. Created in 1959 by Ruth Handler, Barbie gave Mattel domination of this new type of aspirational doll, initially resisted by toy buyers because she had breasts.

A traditional Danish wooden toy company launched Lego (its name deriving from *leg godt* meaning "play well") in 1958, designed by the son of founder Godtfred Christiansen, little knowing that forty years later the firm would be running theme parks devoted to the ubiquitous studded brick.

The toy that convinced a generation that Raphael was a plastic superhero.

Toys grow up, too

Many toy designs were precursors of full-scale versions. In sixteenth-century Holland, children played with toy helicopters. Model hot-air balloons preceded the real thing. Victorian optical toys of the late nineteenth century paved the way for the moving image. The Wright brothers are said to have been inspired by a model plane brought from Paris by their uncle.

The improbably built Barbie, the despair of feminist mothers everywhere.

R2D2 makes his contribution to George Lucas's pension fund.

The march of the plastic people has continued unabated, encouraged by tie-ins with TV cartoons. Remember Transformers, Teenage Mutant Ninja Turtles, Power Rangers…

SEE THE FILM, BUY THE LUNCH BOX…

The tie-in isn't a new idea: it started in 1929 when artist Dick Calkins first drew the Buck Rogers comic strip. Despite the Depression there was a huge demand for the XZ31 Rocket Pistol, which became the hit toy of 1934, to be followed by many variations: spaceships, uniforms, watches, chemistry sets, and all the stationery items you would expect today. Now movie company Lucasfilm expects to make as much money on concessions on tie-ins as from its actual cinematic output.

1971 Intel invents the microprocessor, bringing with it the possibility of drastic reductions in the size of computers.

1972 The Star of Sierra Leone is discovered: weighing in at 969.8 carats, it is the third-largest gem-quality diamond ever found.

1982 Computer hackers manage to break into the U.S.'s top defense computer.

1970~2000

Mac Magic
Computerized type

Who would ever have thought that a few electrons flickering on a screen could change the face of graphic design? But this is what happened in 1984 when Apple brought out the Macintosh 128 and the laser printer. Hundreds of years of printing tradition went down the chute. As the software became more powerful, and image manipulation more sophisticated, new sorts of graphic design became possible.

The Apple IIC by frog, *Time* magazine's design of the year in 1984.

This was the age of postmodernism, and the time was ripe for one of those regular design rethinks. In Basel, design guru *Wolfgang WEINGART* (b.1914) had abandoned the straightjacket of formal Swiss typography for a fresh experimental approach in the 1970s, and his ideas struck a chord with young designers in the U.S. *April GREIMAN* (b.1948) applied these new ideas to computer graphics, and West Coast New Wave was born.

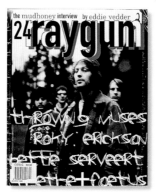

Surf's up, and we're (ray) gunning for you. California style from 1985.

Others immersed in the California culture have followed. *David CARSON* (b.1958), a veteran surfer, turned his *Ray Gun* surfer magazine into the trendiest journal on the newsstand. Husband-and-wife team *Zuzana LICKO* (b.1961) and *Rudy VANDERLANS* (b.1955), respectively Slovakian and Dutch, set up a design consultancy in 1983 and pounced on the Mac when it came out. They used it to design their house journal *Émigré*, which became the byword in trendy typography, exploiting the Mac to create weird and wonderful typefaces.

1984 Canadian writer William Gibson coins the term "cyberspace" in his novel *Neuromancer*.

1987 Britain suffers its worst storm in memory; thousands of trees are knocked down, including the oaks after which the town of Sevenoaks is named.

1996 New York's *Bring in 'Da Noise, Bring in 'Da Funk* is an exciting new musical on Broadway, with its street-style tap and a wide range of American popular music, from swing through rap.

GRAND YOUNG MEN

British graphic design was given a shot in the arm by the bad boys of punk in the 1970s. Their raucous, in-your-face music needed a suitable look, and this was provided by *Jamie* REID (b.1940), with his gritty designs for their record sleeves. It was a reworking of Dada chaos, but with torn collage reminiscent of blackmail notes.

Punk gets to grips with typography in arresting style from 1977.

NEVER MIND THE BOLLOCKS

HERE'S THE

SeX PiSTOLs

In the years that followed, the indie music industry had a close relationship with many advanced ideas in graphics. Magazines were launched that drew on this new talent, aimed at the young "street-style" readership. Two that have survived are Terry Jones's *I-D* and Nick Logan's *The Face*, both launched in 1980.

The Face, elder statesman of style magazines, still trendy after all these years.

THE FACE

ack Dee, Eddie Izzard, and Britain's new comedy

No 43 APRIL 1992 £1.60 • US $4.95

SQUATTING
The end of crusty culture?

BELFAST CLUBBING
United steps of Ireland

SAMOAN GANGSTERS
Fear and loathing in LA control

INNER CITY
Pedro Almodóvar

MIAMI BEACH
America's model world

SOUNDS OF BLACKNESS

SAINT BONO

DEFROCKED

U2
Exclusive in-depth interview

Art directing *The Face* gave *Neville* BRODY (b.1957) an opportunity to try out his radical design ideas on an unsuspecting public. He went on to form Fuse, a group of like-minded typographers who were dedicated to discovering the limits of legibility of type.

1971 London Bridge, first built in 1831, is sold and reassembled in Lake Havasu City.

1977 The world's last known natural case of smallpox is reported on October 26 in Somalia.

1979 More than a million people visit the Picasso Retrospective exhibition at New York's Museum of Modern Art.

1970~2000
Not a Second Time
Retro

A bit of this and a bit of that.

Was postmodernism a post-1945 phenomenon related to consumerism? Many designers say it floated in as Pop Art began to expire, aided and abetted by American architect Robert VENTURI (b. 1925) in his book Complexity and Contradiction in Architecture *(1966). This challenged the Modern movement and all who sailed in her, and supported what one writer has called "eclecticism with integrity." Crudely, Venturi said that architects might pick and choose elements from the art, architecture, and design of the past, and use them as integral features or decor in buildings they thought were "relevant" or "of today."*

Postmodernism is hard to define, but its bizarre and sometimes attractively loopy architectural features are often outstanding. Oscar Wilde wrote that only the really serious can be frivolous. So just where was enigmatic, playful Mr. Venturi coming from? Were his designs simply quoting from the past, or offering a clearly thought-out range of absolute values? He antagonized the over-50s and appealed to youth, but posterity condemned him for being just too knowing.

The 90s' Love Bug, with added oomph for the go-faster hippie.

EVERY HOME SHOULD HAVE ONE

Drive my car

The secret, simple (and new) Beetle. Great retro? The last licensed Volkswagen Beetle had been sold in the U.S. in 1979, and by 1992 the VW name was nearly extinct there. Time for a change. Audi designers Mays and Schreyer secretly resurrected the Beetle, finally gaining approval from their sister company. The new Beetle's sales pitch emphasized its "simple, reliable, honest, and original" properties, and the advertisers hit American youth: "Less flower. More power," "Reverse engineered from UFOs." Herbie (in Disney's *The Love Bug*) would have had a fit.

1983 Swiss-made Swatch watches are launched and prove an immediate hit.

1987 Hungarian-born Italian porn star Ilona Staller (La Cicciolina) is elected to the Italian parliament, campaigning on ecological issues and sexual liberation.

1993 The 150th Grand National steeplechase is abandoned after two false starts.

What a funny chap that Mr. Graves is. Wonder if it makes nice tea...

and metaphor. Quite so. Graves's design followed the famous Bollitore kettle by *Richard SAPPER* (b.1932, Germany) for the same company (1983).

Among other alumni of postmodern design was *Daniel WEIL* (b.1953, Argentina), whose fascinating transparent objects included a radio in a bag (1981; clocks came soon after), to challenge/dispense with hard molding. Bet *James DYSON* (b. 1947) thought about this before making his cylindrical see-through cyclone vacuum cleaner in the 1980s.

One of Venturi's most important followers was the American architect *Michael GRAVES* (b.1934), a fast-learning designer. His Disney Corporation Headquarters in Burbank, California, was a classical temple in reddish pink, columns topped by the Seven Dwarfs holding up the pediment, and a colonnaded water garden in front. Mmm. Graves did domestic stuff, too. His 1985 kettle—for Italy's Alessi—with its whistling bird (yeah: when the water boiled...you got it) is now a postmodern design classic (truly), deemed to have combined narrative

Dyson's cyclone cleaner, an efficient pink phenomenon.

Old style, new materials: Aprilia's Moto 6,5 motorbike by Philippe Starck, 1995.

Retro-chic

It depends who's doing the talking. Is "retro" a revived style of the recent past, or French for "bric-a-brac from any period since Louis XIV"? It can mean modern mass-produced pseudo-objects, like the 100,000 Victorian pub mirrors made each week in Britain during 1977 (why, for heaven's sake?). Or more recently, it can be old games, old Churchill speeches on tape, period burger-bars, or Irish theme pubs. Like postmodernism, retro is drawn from cultural or design memory, communal or personal, and someone's always there to tell you that this is the way it was, and the way it should be remembered.

1983 "Just Say No" is the slogan for a new project to combat drug use unveiled by First Lady Nancy Reagan in October.

1987 Brazilian landowners burn 80,000 square miles of Amazon rainforest in 79 days, prompting fears of a "greenhouse effect" that will increase global temperatures and raise sea levels.

1990 Washington's National Cathedral (Cathedral Church of St. Peter and St. Paul) is completed after 80 years of construction; the Gothic structure is designed by Philip Hubert Frohman.

1980~2000

Mulch

Green design

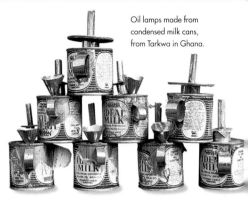

Oil lamps made from condensed milk cans, from Tarkwa in Ghana.

Excuse me… just how eco-friendly are you? Not nearly enough, according to eco-brainstormer Victor PAPANEK (1926–98). In 1971 this Viennese-born American academic wrote Design for the Real World, *an intellectual's soapbox disguised as a book. It's still with us. During the 1950s and 60s, Papanek was associated with Vance Packard and Ralph Nader, shrill critics of less pleasant associations between advertising and consumerism, and orchestrators of increasing mistrust felt around the world toward the large corporations that had learned to advertise and sell consumers mutton dressed as lamb.*

One result was that consumer organizations began to flourish, and the concept of the "best buy" came home to roost. After all, why throw good money at trash? *Design for the Real World* pointed at the general failure of Western Europe and North America to deal with the waste they create. Avarice (So what's with the planet? Let's profit!) gets in the way. It was influential, published as the hippie movement's right-on promotion of recycling; junk culture began to wane. Here was a respectable academic (not a long-haired freak, right?) with design ideas to make ornery people think about social responsibility, design, the planet, and alternatives. Your mind should be open to the total revision of…well, your lifestyle.

Best buys
America's Consumer Union began in 1936. Britain's Consumer Association is an animal of 1957, and now a pressure group to be reckoned with.

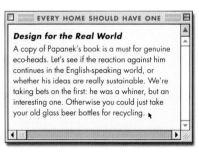

☐ ≡≡≡ EVERY HOME SHOULD HAVE ONE ≡≡ ▤
Design for the Real World
A copy of Papanek's book is a must for genuine eco-heads. Let's see if the reaction against him continues in the English-speaking world, or whether his ideas are really sustainable. We're taking bets on the first: he was a whiner, but an interesting one. Otherwise you could just take your old glass beer bottles for recycling.

1993 Vikram Seth's novel *A Suitable Boy* becomes the longest novel (1,000 pages) in English in 245 years.

1995 France conducts nuclear tests beneath atolls southeast of Tahiti, breaking a 1992 test moratorium.

1996 *Pravda* ceases publication after losing millions of dollars for the two Greek businessmen who bought it in 1992.

LOOKS AREN'T EVERYTHING

Sometimes it's hard to separate "green" from "commonsense" with Papanek. He did believe firmly in putting Function before Form. Make it suitable for its purpose before worrying about its good looks. This was the man who made a transistor radio out of tin cans to prove ease of cheap manufacture in developing countries. He pointed out (quite rightly) that too many knobs and switches on hi-fi systems confused the elderly, and suggested that self-assembly products were good because buyers could adapt them for their own needs.

Papanek's design work for UNESCO in the Third World, and the World Health Organization, is almost predictable. But let's be clear: he was flawed, and could be tiresome, lightweight, and plain wrong, for all his peers and thousands of supporters, including princes and millionaires. Money doesn't always change those nasty habits.

GREEN BIBLE

Green commerce really caught on during the 1980s. Cosmetics led the way, increasing awareness of the dangers of chlorofluorocarbons in aerosols and of products tested on animals. In the 1990s the promoters of organic foods quickly caught up, when medically related issues (BSE, or "mad cow disease") and food scares (genetically modified foodstuffs) made their products a real alternative.

Organic produce benefited from the food hygiene scares of the 90s.

Vroom, vroom

Think green, think fuel, and learn to loathe the internal combustion engine, aviation spirit, and anything else that propels mankind and pollutes the atmosphere or the oceans in the process. The alternatives are pack animals, sailing ships, or bicycles? No, sorry, alternative fuels aren't a proper answer. Gas and coke have been used before, but only under pressure.

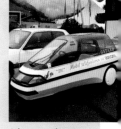

Solar-powered cars: is this what we will be driving into the future?

Vancouver taxis switched to natural gas in 1989, but the best natural gas to use is hydrogen, which is just a little combustible. What about BMW Technik's BMW Z1? Weren't they talking about degradable parts in the 1980s?

Electric cars have made hopeful if irregular appearances. In 1996 the DB NECAR switched on and made it to 70mph. Great, but what about the power source? If you're going to do it properly, you have to get it from solar panels or wind turbines. A nasty nuclear power station takes up no space at all compared with the acres you need for a solar farm. And as for a wind farm—oy vey! An orgy of noise, for miles and miles. And don't tell me that the engine design, the exhaust clean-up, and the fuel quality won't leave deposits of some sort, somewhere on the asphalt...

But how do you know what's good for you? You need a bible—of sorts. In September 1988 *The Green Consumer Guide* by British greens John Elkington and Julia Hailes was published.

By January 1989 it was into its eighth printing. Proof of a green pudding...

1980 A huge boom in fitness takes place, and aerobics becomes the latest exercise craze.

1982 Scientists transfer a growth-controlling gene from a rat to a mouse, which then doubles in size.

1984 British ice-dance duo Christopher Dean and Jayne Torvill win a gold medal for their performance at the Winter Olympics.

1980~2000
Bladerunners
Sports gear

And show 'em your chest, your shorts, your socks...Very near you right now there's someone with a designer's name on themselves. On their bosom or their manly chest, or nerdlike on a reversed baseball cap. And especially on training shoes (of course, you know the makers; let's not give them any more publicity).

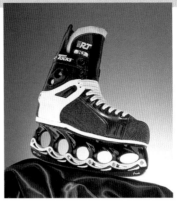

The Würthner t'blade, frog's tungsten steel skate blade, state-of-the-art and super-cool.

EVERY HOME SHOULD HAVE ONE

Run!

...at least one pair of Nike Air trainers, or Reebok Classics. Too un-trendy? Think about how they got to be where they are. And if you don't want to run, and biking is your thing, then buy an expensive mountain bike and do whatever it takes. For charity, of course.

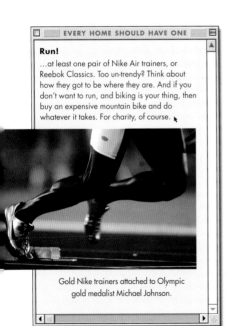

Gold Nike trainers attached to Olympic gold medalist Michael Johnson.

Sportswear became a late-twentieth-century design phenomenon because the designer labels gave it status, and because professional teams began to receive big business sponsorship. The sponsor's name had to appear somewhere, so why not on the team's uniform? Ralph Lauren chose "Polo" because he loves England and wanted a sporty name, not because ponies roam wild in Manhattan.

TREAD CAREFULLY

The worst culprits in this grim tale of exploitation are the training and running-shoe makers. Too many, too often. Parents have fought battles worse than Waterloo or the Alamo with their kids because of peer group pressure to buy this or that brand of shoe...to those who held out, we salute you. The chain-store brand wouldn't do? Surprise, surprise.

1986 30 million people take part in sponsored events worldwide to raise money for Bob Geldof's Sport Aid.

1994 British film *Four Weddings and a Funeral* is an unexpected hit on both sides of the Atlantic, reaching the No. 1 position in the U.S.

1998 Ginger Spice leaves the Spice Girls, and two of the remaining members announce they are pregnant.

Trainers appeared in the 1970s because jogging for weight loss became a habit of epidemic proportions. And because any long-distance walk or run can cause percussion injuries when heels and arches repeatedly strike the ground, special shoes were devised. After all, no one's tootsies are the same. Real designers thought real thoughts, for gravel or grass, but everything blurred: soon every trainer maker offered something different.

And if you're interested in this gear only so you can look cool (millions fall into this category), you want the best. For "best," read "most expensive" or "most heavily hyped." Air heels. This sole. That color. This cushioning. The other padding. Ever been had? Not to mention the sailing or boat shoes offered as universal casual wear for the young and not so young.

THE WILD FRONTIER?

Sports of the 80s and 90s like mountain-biking, skiing, and skate- and snowboarding have different ergonomic problems. So...each has its wardrobe. Be a distressed astronaut in a silvery padded ski jacket. Or a pair of drafty but sporty airfield windsocks with legs for the spins, ollies, flips, and board-grabs of skate- or snowboarding. And for the Rockies foothills, why not truss yourself in an outdoor version of something out of Marvel Comics, complete with designer labels?

WHO LOVES YA?

The ad men, of course. You have to be designer fodder: a "geezer," 16–25 years old, living in an urban location (read "inner city"). Which presumably means that you wear designer sportswear (monogrammed shirt flapping over sportswear trousers or side-buttoned striped joggers, with "name" trainers endorsed by your favorite sportsperson) because you want to escape from the Alcatraz of daily life.

The great outdoors, where the clothes are as exciting as the sport.

> ### Learning the game
> OK, suckers, how about this. In 1999 one British university offered a BA course in fashion (Sportswear and Streetwear). That means clothes "...that reflect the need of non-mainstream groups ...that reflect the move away from dressier styles ...that give a strong identity to a sub-culture ...that blur the lines of gender." God help us.

1982 MRI (Magnetic Resonance Imaging) machines introduced in Britain give physicians a superior new diagnostic tool, permitting them to monitor soft tissue and fluids, as well as bone.

1987 U.S. Surgeon General C. Everett Koop advises a House subcommitee to permit condom commercials on TV to help stop the AIDS epidemic.

1989 San Francisco is hit by North America's most destructive earthquake since 1906: the tremors buckle highways and the Bay Bridge, killing an estimated 90 people.

1980~2000

Gotcha!

Designer wars

In the competitive global trading environment that has developed in the last thirty years, image is all. Big business has come to realize how important design is in the battle for our hearts and wallets. As the desire for market share sharpens competition, design has become a major selling point, incorporating a company's identity through packaging and advertising. Vast sums are invested in winning the design battle.

Nowhere can this be seen more clearly than in the great cola conflict. PepsiCo took a bold step toward challenging the Coca-Cola company's world domination in 1996 when it broke the unwritten rule that cola cans should be red (but diet cola, white). To make a distinct break from market leader Coke, it relaunched its redesigned blue can with a $400 million publicity campaign. This included repainting the Concorde in the new Pepsi identity and the first commercial shot in space by the Mir cosmonauts, which featured a giant Pepsi can floating in space—at a reported cost of $2 million.

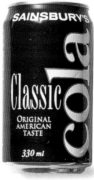

When the British supermarket chain Sainsbury's launched its own-brand cola in 1992, it "borrowed" some of Coke's famous style. Threatened with legal action, Sainsbury's changed the design, but not before it had benefited from a lot of publicity. ASDA supermarkets was taken to court in Britain in 1994 by a cookie company for infringing the copyright of the latter's well-known packaging with a lookalike pack of its own. ASDA lost the case.

Hands off! Sainsbury's cola, before (bottom) and after the design changes demanded by Coke's lawyers.

> **Packaging is powerful**
>
> When the Michael Peters Company redesigned the traditional packaging of Winsor & Newton's colored inks in 1982, by packaging the bottles in colorful illustrated boxes, a different one for each color, sales increased by 400 percent.

1991 A Bronze Age corpse in an incredible state of preservation is discovered in the Austrian Alps.

1992 Italians are estimated to consume an average of 70 liters of wine per person per year.

1995 The Rock-and-Roll Hall of Fame opens in Cleveland in a building on Lake Erie designed by I. M. Pei.

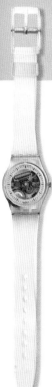

Swatch's jelly watch, meant to be ephemeral, yet eminently collectible.

SUCK MY CARPET

Many designers and inventors have been rebuffed by established manufacturers. Black & Decker turned down Ron Hickman's Workmate folding workbench. The company recanted after he patented it, and it has since sold over twenty million. James Dyson met a distinct lack of interest from some major electrical companies when he showed them his revolutionary bagless vacuum cleaner in the early 1980s. He subsequently struggled to get it made under license and finally manufactured it himself. It has since become an icon—not only designed well inside, but with an expressively functional outer casing: distinctly postmodern. By 1994 his original upright DC01 model became the biggest-selling cleaner in Britain. In 1999, swallowing its pride, Hoover Europe launched, yes, a bagless "vortex" vacuum cleaner.

WATCH WARS

In the early 1980s, the Swiss watch industry was reeling from the onslaught of the Far East's electronic watch revolution. How did they strike back? In 1983 Thomke, Muller, and Mock created the brilliant concept of the Swatch watch: high-tech, mass-produced, and streetwise. Originally intended to be disposable, in fact they became collectible through a stream of strap and face designs, many designed by famous names.

Now Swatch has had the cheek to redesign time. Its Beat watch claims to be Internet time—the same worldwide for everyone, the first watch of the virtual cyberage! The day has been divided up into a thousand beats, each representing 86.4 seconds.

EVERY HOME SHOULD HAVE ONE

iMac

Everyone thought the writing was on the wall for Apple Computer in the mid-90s, overwhelmed by the price advantage of the many IBM-compatible PCs that ran on Microsoft's software. And then along came the iMac. Created by Apple's design team, headed by British designer Jonathan Ive (b.1968), it broke the mold of the bland beige box with its fresh-looking translucent blue case, and became an instant "design classic."

The complete rainbow of iMac flavors.

1979 Britain's annual Fastnet yacht race in the English Channel and Irish Sea ends in disaster as gale-force winds and huge waves hit more than 600 boats, drowning 15 sailors.

1981 The musical *Cats* opens in London with lyrics by poet T.S. Eliot and music by Andrew Lloyd Webber.

1985 The wreck of the *Titanic* is discovered off Newfoundland at a depth of 13,200 feet.

1970~2000

Boys' Toys

Gadgets

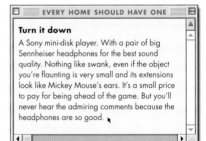

The 1999 iBook from Apple, for boys who work on the run.

In the 60s a portable transistor radio was good, but an 8-track player in a car was better. In the 70s the pocket calculator reigned supreme, closely followed by the digital watch. The 80s saw the mobile phone contest the market with the Sony Walkman. And the 90s? Apple's iMac, perhaps, or a DVD of some sort. And what do all these have to do with each other? Why, they're all Boys' Toys! The things that men can't resist buying so they can show off to other men (or women). And when they tire of these things, they'll buy something else that looks good and snappy and is fresh on display.

Toys for boys aren't especially new. Mr. Toad of *Wind in the Willows* had a skiff, a canary-colored cart, and a motorcar in swift succession, and other, human Toads have followed suit. Toys are like jewelry,

> **EVERY HOME SHOULD HAVE ONE**
>
> **Turn it down**
>
> A Sony mini-disk player. With a pair of big Sennheiser headphones for the best sound quality. Nothing like swank, even if the object you're flaunting is very small and its extensions look like Mickey Mouse's ears. It's a small price to pay for being ahead of the game. But you'll never hear the admiring comments because the headphones are so good.

made to be exhibited. In the auto department you can name 'em yourself. Porsche. BMW. Harley Davidson.

Other obvious toys are divers' watches (try Omega) and cameras, though the latter are a little more difficult. The Polaroid Land Camera (1947), named after its inventor *Edwin LAND* (1909–91),

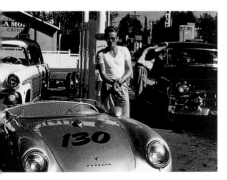

James Dean with his classy but ill-fated Porsche. Not really a toy after all.

was a fine example, but since then we've had the Olympus Trip (1968), a host of

1987 World population reaches five billion, double the figure for 1950.

1990 Junk bond king Michael Milken pleads guilty to insider trading.

1995 Holy statues around the world develop a taste for milk as reports flood in of Hindu religious statues sipping up to 20 liters of the stuff.

single-lens reflex cameras with auto-focusing zoom lenses, and immediate classics like the small Canon Ixus (1996). No self-respecting Boy could possibly turn away from a camcorder (for about five minutes), and in 1999 the Viewcam is with us, a video camera compatible with computer software.

Speaking of which, boys' toys are rather more interesting when they're allied to business. Why have personal organizers supplanted diaries? You will know why when you think about your bulging Filofax, another ridiculous 80s arrival: because personal organizers are as small as your hand, and crammed with data. In terms of miniaturism, those wretched pagers that squeal and play silly tunes are nearly as bad. Plus the mobile phones that keep shrinking.

Rather bigger, and now capable of handling a modem and DVD without any hassle is the laptop PC. One of the most useful boys' toys of the 1990s, it's been around for a while, has really proved its worth, and any monied youth can have one. Dare one mention pens in the same breath? A Mont Blanc fountain pen's the thing that ostentatious boys will want to have on view in the office, even if they use it only to sign their name. Some bauble. There's no serious competitor—not even the Parker Duofold (1994).

Mont Blanc Meisterstück 149— top of the world.

Lighten up
The Tizio table lamp (1972) by Richard Sapper (b.1932) is still a great favorite. Made of lightweight aluminum with counterweights, it was one of the first of its kind to use a halogen bulb as a spotlight. It's just one of many descendants of the famous 1933 Anglepoise by George Carwardine (1887–1948).

Fully posable and entirely cable-free, the Tizio is the acme of elegant illumination.

LIGHTING-UP TIME!
Boys' toys include lots of designer furniture, and desk lamps and accessories have always been favorites, at work or at home. Japanese design is great in the office, and there are too many designers to list. But every desk needs its storage caddy, and many attractive and innovative drawer sets and containers come from this quarter. Of course, if all you want to do is sit around and watch TV, the boy's best buy is probably one of Philippe Starck's designs for the Thomson Group. Their unusual casings are something else. And you can use one of his clocks to check the program timing, too. In case you miss The Next Big Thing, of course.

1978 Soviet authorities permit a Moscow exhibition of avant-garde paintings, but only after a score of works have been removed for ideological reasons.

1979 Rock-and-roll musician Chuck Berry is jailed for three months for evading taxes.

1986 A law makes it illegal for American hospitals to turn away patients who can no longer afford to pay, but nearly a third of Americans have inadequate health insurance or none at all.

1975~2000

Wired, Weird, and Wonderful
Computer games

Computers have two aspects—hardware and software—and each requires very different design approaches. The digital age took the sages by surprise—no one predicted the World Wide Web. Its creator, British scientist Tim Berners-Lee, saw it as means of convenient academic communication. It was a creaky system until a computer with a graphical interface came along—i.e., enough memory for pictures—and we haven't looked back. Some say that the Internet is the most important thing since the flushing toilet. Discuss.

ZAP THOSE ALIENS

Parents used to complain about their children hanging around in amusement arcades—now they complain about them being at home gazing at their computer screens, playing "arcade" games for hours on end. About 25 years ago, the numbingly dull game *Pong* swept the pubs and clubs of the world, and it seemed remarkable that twisting a knob made a shape move up or down on the black-and-white screen. How far things have come! How much better was Taito Corporation's 1978 *Space Invaders*, only to be bettered by Namco's *PacMan*.

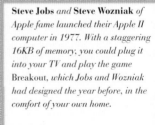

One of the earliest hand-held Nintendo games from the 80s.

DESIGNER NAMES

Steve Jobs *and* **Steve Wozniak** *of Apple fame launched their Apple II computer in 1977. With a staggering 16KB of memory, you could plug it into your TV and play the game* Breakout, *which Jobs and Wozniak had designed the year before, in the comfort of your own home.*

DESIGNER NAMES

1990 The Internet, created by the National Science Foundation in 1985, replaces the military network begun in 1969.

1994 Pop star Michael Jackson marries Lisa-Marie Presley.

1996 U.S. biochemist Shannon Lucid spends six months in the Russian space station Mir, setting a new record for an American astronaut.

A succession of more complex and more graphically impressive games have followed, as the big three, Sega, Nintendo, and Sony, battle it out. Game consoles are becoming more powerful: the Sega Dreamcast can double as a PC, with direct connection to the Internet, and like other digital devices will probably merge into a single multipurpose computing and entertainment device.

Games designers are a recent breed. Software designers used to be research scientists. Now they are bright kids who have to know what the latest technology, or the next technology, will be able to do. Companies like Eidos have marched from bedrooms to boardrooms in a few years, challenging the music industry in turnover. Its creation Lara Croft is an example of the influence of game culture. She has become an icon in her own right, and even features in soft-drink advertisements, so that even if you aren't familiar with her unlikely proportions from playing *Tomb Raider*, you will see them on the billboard.

The Internet is fast developing as the domain in which game players blast each other remotely. They may be thousands of miles apart, but they are experiencing the same effects in a virtual, synthetic, designed world.

Forget the camera?

Nintendo stunned the toy industry in 1997 when it launched a mini monochrome camera that could be plugged into the GameBoy, and to go with it, a micro printer that produced postage-stamp-sized prints. Now the grownups can join in the fun— Sony's VAIO C1 notebook computer has a 180° camera in the lid that can take still and video pictures. Digital image technology is developing apace, and the days of the traditional camera are numbered.

The GameBoy camera, for happy snapping in the twenty-first century.

BIG PLAYERS

Nintendo gained 25 million users worldwide with its handheld GameBoy, which began in 1987 with *Tetris*, making its Russian designer, Alexey Pajitnov, famous for 15 months. In 1996 Sony hit the console game market by launching the PlayStation. Designed by Ken Kutaragi, now vice-president of Sony Computer Entertainment, it has become the most successful consumer product ever, selling 50 million units in three years (fortunate for Sony, which had sunk $500 million into the project). And the even more powerful PlayStation 2 is waiting in the wings.

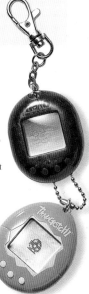

Tamagotchi, the ideal pet for the kid in a hurry.

1950 Polaroid replaces its 1947 sepia print with a black-and-white one, but it is found that the new print fades easily.

1966 China's universities close down under the Cultural Revolution.

1973 American textile mills produce a record 820 million square yards of cotton denim as demand booms for blue jeans and denim jackets.

1940~2000

Hi and Very Fi
Audio

Put a CD into the tray…and remember Émile Berliner's mechanical wind-up disk player (1886). It paved the way for Philips's and Sony's little silver disk (1979) in its jewel case, and for DDM too…but we digress.

The wind-up gramophone's place in modern society was ensured by 1920, and soon afterward the 78 rpm disk was being played on hand-wound gramophones everywhere. Electrical recording began in 1925, when Joseph Maxwell used a microphone to record sound. In 1940 *Billboard* magazine began to compile charts of best-sellers, and in 1948 Columbia made a plastic long-playing record, using a speed of 33⅓ rpm. The same year RCA followed suit with a 45 rpm microgroove disk. The album and the single had arrived.

Singles: remember them? Three minutes of heaven for less than a dollar. They don't make 'em like that any more…

TWO EARS GOOD, FOUR EARS BETTER
Stereophonic sound was developed by EMI in Britain in the 1930s, but you couldn't buy stereo records until 1958. Even then, there were some who wanted surround-sound: they had to wait until 1971 for quadrophonic systems (using four speakers). Ear boggling, baby.

Suddenly, popular music had exploded. Cover art sold albums galore. It was eons away from the 1920s' decorated cardboard album covers, but somehow still connected. Jazz was and still is a great medium for graphic design and artwork: Verve cover photography, 70s CBS, the classic all-over Blue Note concepts, and rarefied ECM are still very special. Hey, be hip, carry one of these 12-inch squares of cardboard under your arm, and show your exquisite taste.

1986 The U.S. Food and Drug Administration approves the first genetically engineered vaccine; it will be used to immunize against hepatitis B.

1991 There are riots in Los Angeles after the police are videotaped beating up an African-American driver, Rodney King.

1999 A computer virus named Melissa that spreads via e-mail closes down hundreds of American computer systems within days.

CDS: SOME YOU WIN

CDs are actually the least degradable of all the recording surfaces invented, but when you're fed up with the album, it'll make a great coaster for your bourbon. These aluminum plates are covered with micro-cells called "pits," which are then played by passing a laser across the disk and sending a signal back to the player. The CD first reached Europe in 1987 (the Japanese had them in 1982) and caused all kinds of dismay. Some found the sound re-mastered from old vinyl records too clean or too sharp, and it's certainly true that originals sound very different (and scratchier, too). But the technology is ever-changing, and eventually even the British will be able to buy CDs at a reasonable price.

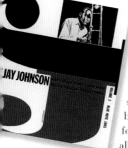

Under graphic designer Reid Miles, Blue Note's record covers were works of art. Listen to the music and put the sleeve on the wall.

The shell-like beauty of B&W's Nautilus speakers.

EVERY HOME SHOULD HAVE ONE

Double hearing

... an example of Bang & Olufsen's hi-fi equipment. This Danish firm has been innovative for decades, and is still style leader in the field. Its catalog of record and CD players is seriously cool, and remains outstanding against all the Asian competition. What's more, it's eco-considerate.

DESIGNER NAMES

Cool sounds? Without Rickenbacker's pioneering electric guitar (California, 1931), no McGuinn (Roger McGuinn of the Byrds, OK?). No outfit is without the Fender electric bass guitar (1950s), and someone in most self-respecting bands plays Fender's guitar classic, the solid-bodied six-string Stratocaster (designed 1952, produced 1954)...well, let's go beetle-browed (sorry, no pun intended) and paraphrase Cézanne speaking of Monet: only a sound, but what a sound. Or as Hendrix once said, "Move over, Rover..."

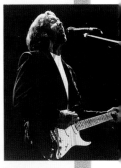

Eric Clapton gives his Stratocaster some hammer.

DESIGNER NAMES

2003 The Internet can now be accessed through any telephone.

2018 Contraceptive chocolate is marketed with a choice of fillings.

2022 Monica Lewinsky becomes the first woman president of the United States.

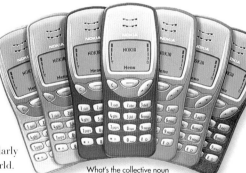

2000 and beyond
Virtually Anything
A designed future

Who needs designers?

Will designers be needed in the future? Computer programs have been written that can generate a series of design possibilities—a development of software designed by William LATHAM (b.1948) that he used to create fantastic alien biomorphic virtual sculptures in the 1980s when sponsored by IBM. You feed in the basic parameters, and the machine evolves a series of designs. If you don't like the look of something it comes up with, ask it to pour out some more permutations. When you get the result you want, send it to the rapid prototyping machine: presto, a new design.

CONVERGING TECHNOLOGIES

Digital technology is going to cause devices that we are familiar with to merge, and this will be a design challenge. The computer, TV, and VCR will soon merge together into a single device. The mobile telephone will become an ancillary device that will enable you to talk to, and see, anyone similarly equipped, from anywhere in the world. Combine it with a global positioning device, and it will be able to tell where you are, too.

What's the collective noun for Nokias? An interruption, a cacophony, a mob...

Nokia (based in Finland, which has the highest mobile phone usage in the world—nearly 60 percent) is developing its next-generation phones to have a keypad, dictionary, and message-sending facilities that will enable them to double as palmtop or PC notebook. A new generation of wireless information devices, WIDs, is being developed that will allow convenient mobile connection to the Internet.

2034 A bionic man is created using donated organs; scientists name him Bill.

2078 Penguins become extinct due to the melting of the Antarctic ice cap.

2095 The price of vacations on the Moon is drastically reduced due to lack of demand.

A mini Mercedes?

POCKET CAR

The car of tomorrow will be small. A new breed of low-emission, small-engined cars is already making an impact in Japan and Europe, pioneered in France by Ligier and the MMC Smart Car. These microcars are ideal for city use and very economical to run. Governments are already introducing tax incentives to encourage their use, and at 90 mpg (644 kmpl) the savings are obvious as oil stocks diminish.

Mercedes has shown the way with its diminutive "A" class minicar. While these would seem laughable on an American highway, there will be changes there, too, as reduced-emission cars become compulsory. The most likely result will be a hybrid-engined car, combining electric with conventional power. And experiments are underway for a hydrogen-powered car that emits only steam.

Electronic pets are easy to keep —if they step out of line, just turn them off.

WHAT NEXT?

Advances in electronics and materials will make new designs possible. Advances in genetic engineering may even make it possible to create biological machines. To recycle them, you could just put them on the compost pile—or perhaps that would be unwise. The biological computer with neurons rather than circuits may make silicon chips redundant and achieve that sci-fi goal of artificial intelligence. Yes, in the future you may be able to have an intelligent conversation with your toaster; wouldn't that be nice?

Of course, all this supposes that we will need physical things. Cyberspace beckons, and if we can afford the time and the VR helmet, perhaps we will get by with pictures in our heads. But then, of course, someone will have to design the pictures...

Battle of the robots

The long-predicted household robot will probably never be perfected, but most household equipment will become intelligent. The refrigerator that keeps track of its contents and reorders provisions is being tested now. Robotic toys and pets are already with us. The toy craze of 1998, the Furby, showed that kids are happy to have an electronic chum. When Sony launched its 3,000 limited edition of Aibo, its robot dog, it sold them all in 20 minutes at $2,066 each. Significantly, you could buy them only through the Net.

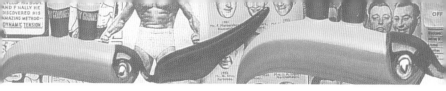

Design Classics

The designation "classic" is offered with such reckless abandon that the cautious reader would do well to treat all such claims with skepticism. However, given this caveat, we have assembled a list of Things that even the most jaundiced critic would have to acknowledge as outstanding responses to design problems in terms of visual impact, or sheer longevity.

Colt revolver.

COLT REVOLVER

If one product marked the arrival of mass-production techniques it was Samuel Colt's design for a handgun with a rotating breech—a stunningly original concept. He carved the first one in wood while away at sea, and patented it in 1853. He was able to employ the most modern engineering skills, and by 1860 he was running the most advanced arms factory in the world.

THONET CHAIR

It is remarkable that one of the design classics of the twentieth century was devised by a man born in the eighteenth century. Michael Thonet had a wonderfully simple concept that combined new technology (bending wood) and simple,

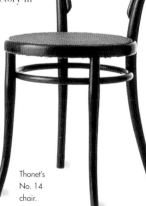

Thonet's No. 14 chair.

effective design. His 1859 No. 14 chair became one of the most successful products ever made, the café and school-hall chair of the world. By 1930, 50 million had been made.

GILLETTE RAZOR

The cutthroat razor dated back to Roman times, but in 1895 King Camp Gillette, a salesman, realized that only a sliver of metal was needed to do the job, and with the engineer William Nickerson he designed a disposable product that was to make shaving a much more convenient process. In 1902 they patented it as the "Safety" Razor, and after initial resistance founded what became a multinational company.

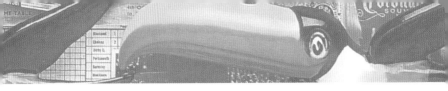

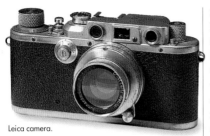

Leica camera.

LONDON UNDERGROUND MAP

Harry Beck was an engineer who worked for the London Transport Board. Using his knowledge of electrical wiring diagrams, he designed a non-geographical map of the underground train system in 1931. It was refined over the next twenty-five years, and its principle copied all over the world.

LEICA CAMERA

Oskar Barnack's 1913 design for a small, convenient hand-held camera revolutionized not only the shape and size of the camera, but also the nature of what could be photographed. The 35mm camera remains one of the most outstanding and consistently developed products of the twentieth century, and yet it was originally designed to test movie film.

CARTIER TANK WATCH

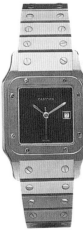

Louis Cartier was a jewelry designer to the rich and famous. The wristwatch had been a popular item of ladies' jewelry long before World War I, but Cartier, inspired by the rugged shape of the new war machine, the tank, saw the possibility of creating a more macho wristwatch in the early 1920s, breaking the long tradition of a circular watch forever.

Cartier Tank Watch.

B32 CANTILEVER CHAIR

Coke bottle.

Although he didn't invent the concept of the tubular steel chair frame (Mart Stam had already done that), Marcel Breuer refined the idea after several experiments (he was said to have been inspired by the handlebars of his bicycle). He achieved a brilliant combination of chromed steel tubing with caned seat and back in his B32 chair of 1928. Much imitated, this classic design has been in constant production ever since.

COKE BOTTLE

The famous waisted Coke bottle, designed by Alexander Samuelson, became part of the Coca-Cola company's marketing effort in 1915. Even at this time, Coke was spending $1 million a year on publicity and advertising. It is now so associated with Coke's image that a picture of the bottle is printed on the cans.

Anglepoise lamp.

ANGLEPOISE LAMP

Some designers are prolific, but we know George Carwardine only for his brilliant Anglepoise desk lamp, originally made by spring makers Terry & Co. The lamp that goes were you want works with counterbalancing springs that mimic the muscles in the human arm. It has been in constant production since 1934 with only slight changes.

VW BEETLE

Born out of Hitler's desire to give every German citizen a car, the Volkswagen (literally, people's car) was a radical concept that combined a rear air-cooled engine in a streamlined body shell. It was designed by Ferdinand Porsche, who, with his son, went on to design the famous production sports cars.

VESPA SCOOTER

The Vespa (Italian for wasp), born out of postwar Italian reconstruction, was the brainchild of industrialist Enrico Piaggio, given form by his engineer Corradino D'Ascanio, an aircraft engineer, who incorporated new technology into a streamlined body shell. Launched in 1946, the Vespa and its competitors brought style to the face of two-wheeled transportation, and helped revive Italy's reputation for inspired automotive design and engineering.

Vespa

VW Beetle.

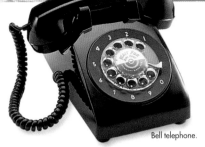

MOUSE

There was a time, not so long ago, when all the instructions for a computer had to be put in using the keyboard. The useful add-on to your computer known as a "mouse" was first designed by Douglas Englebart in 1968 while he was working at the Stanford Research Institute. It didn't become well known until 1984, when it came as standard with the Apple Mac. Now 90 million are made every year, in all shapes and sizes.

iMac mouse.

Bell telephone.

BELL 500 TELEPHONE

In 1946 Henry Dreyfuss was commissioned by Bell Telephones to update its standard telephone, the 302, which he had designed in 1937. The result was the 1949 "500," a clean-lined, modern handset that became the standard form of the telephone worldwide until the changes of the 1970s. It was much imitated and (rather like the early Fords) was available only in black, until 1953, when the "fashion" phone started to be promoted.

HELVETICA TYPEFACE

You see Helvetica every day of your life, probably without realizing it. This one-off design was created in 1957 by Edouard Hoffman and Max Miedinger for the Haas type foundry, where Miedinger was the in-house designer. It was a reworking of traditional sans serif types, but with an elegance that was lacking in the harsher geometric designs of the 30s. Helvetica is a "neutral" design, which makes it appropriate for use in many design situations, but particularly corporate design and signage.

Helvetica.

Attractive. Reliable. Economical.
The new VW 1600s.
Bigger and better value for money.

only

1

...s company ...fordable...

first direct

Design Heroes

It takes a certain kind of heroism (or egomania, take your pick) to offer your ideas up for public consumption (or rejection—remember the Sinclair C5?) Here we present some of the stars of the design firmament who were bold enough to make the world the way they wanted it.

PETER BEHRENS (GER.) 1869–1940

Although he trained as a painter, Behrens became a versatile designer and pioneer of the concept of a corporate identity when he worked for the AEG company as artistic director from 1905. He was equally at home designing factories, kettles, furniture, light fixtures, or bookbindings. Key twentieth-century figures such as Le Corbusier, Gropius, and Mies van der Rohe worked in his office in the 1910s.

Behrens nickel-plated kettle, 1909.

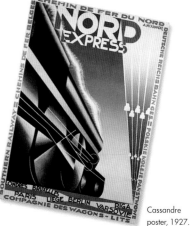

Cassandre poster, 1927.

A. M. CASSANDRE (FRA.) 1901–1968

Born Adolphe Jean-Marie Mouron, Cassandre adopted his pseudonym when he was engulfed by the climate of artistic ideas after his arrival in Paris in 1915. He designed his first poster in 1923 and quickly became famed for his striking travel posters. His cubist, geometric style with bold typography was very much in keeping with the modern mood of the time, expressive of the jazz age.

KENNETH GRANGE (U.K.) B.1929

Grange is Britain's most respected product designer, with a long record of producing well-thought-out, appropriate, and user-friendly designs. He made his name with the redesign of the Kenwood food mixer in 1960, and also updated the Brownie camera for Kodak.

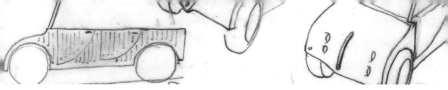

He was a founding member in 1972 of the influential Pentagram design consultancy, which has since been responsible for raising the standards of British product design, graphic design, and architecture. He is probably best known for his cab design for the British Rail 125 high-speed train.

EILEEN GRAY (IRELAND) 1878–1976

Born to an aristocratic Irish family, Eileen Gray spent all her working life in France. Although her work was never mass-produced, her elegant furniture designs were an original combination of restrained modernism and traditional craft skills, particularly the Japanese lacquering techniques that she mastered. She excelled with folding screens, exotic combinations of materials, and the clever use of storage space in furniture. The simple geometry of much of her work associates it with the Art Deco style.

JOSEF HOFFMANN
(CZECH./AUS.) 1870–1956

Hoffmann trained as an architect, but then flourished in the ferment of ideas that were in the air in the 1890s, becoming a founding member of the Vienna Secession. His visual ideas were in step with other innovators like Charles Rennie Mackintosh, and he was a prolific designer of furniture, textiles, and metalwork. His architectural work was strikingly modern, and his exhibition pavilions gave his work a wide audience.

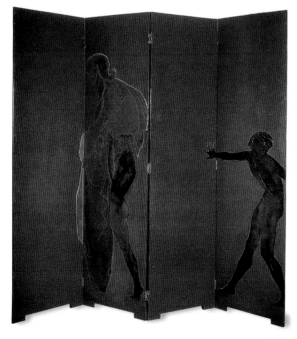

Le Destin, a four-paneled lacquered screen designed by Eileen Gray in 1914.

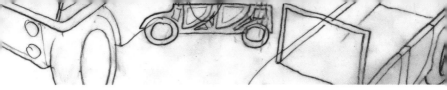

RAYMOND LOEWY
(FRA./U.S.) **1893–1986**
Loewy is recognized as
one of the significant
figures who made U.S.
manufacturers aware of
product design, starting
his career in the 1930s
despite the Depression.
He was aware of the
importance of styling,
adopting streamlining
as a modern style to be applied
to a wide variety of products. An
accomplished self-publicist with offices
in nine cities, he and his team were
responsible for a huge range of products,
from the famous Lucky Strike pack
redesign of 1941 to the Skylab interiors
for NASA in the 1960s and 70s.

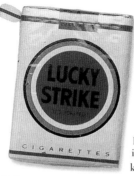

Lucky Strike pack, 1941.

DIETER RAMS (GER.) **B.1932**
Rams had training in both architecture and
carpentry, and developed a clear,
minimalist design philosophy that
blossomed with his work as designer
at Braun, where he was design
director from 1960 to
1980. He showed that
humble consumer goods
like hairdryers and
razors could have a
design esthetic without
decoration, and that
design applied to the
whole object, not just
the exterior.

PAUL RAND (U.S.) **1914–96**
A New Yorker, whose long
and impressive career greatly
influenced the direction of
American graphic design. He
was strongly influenced by the
ideas of European modernism
as a student, and made his
mark with a new style of
photomontaged magazine cover
in the 1930s and 40s. His best-
known work is the logo and
corporate style he developed for
IBM in 1956. His writings have
meant he has been able to spread his
design philosophy to a younger generation.

ETTORE SOTTSASS (AUS./ITAL.) **B.1917**
Sottsass has been a leading figure in Italian
design for four decades. Starting as an
architect in 1946, he quickly diversified
into furniture and ceramics, and then with
product design work for Olivetti
Electronics. He has continually refreshed
his ideas through travel and by being open
to new influences, and has been an
inspiration to radical designers.
He is best known
for the informal association
of the Memphis group, which
popularized postmodernism in
the 1980s, and has
continually surprised with
novel work in new materials.

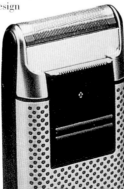

Braun electric razor.

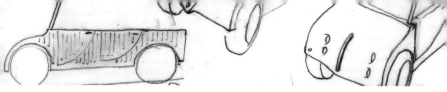

PHILIPPE STARCK (FRA.) B.1949

With a mixture of architecture and fashion in his backround, Starck found himself enjoying the status of a superstar in the 1980s "design decade," when he came to the notice of President Mitterand and was hired to redesign his private rooms. He has since produced a flow of innovative products, furniture, interiors, and architecture, with buildings now in Tokyo, Paris, and Antwerp, but is probably best known to the general public for the spiky lemon squeezer and toothbrush that typify his very personal design approach.

Starck lemon squeezer.

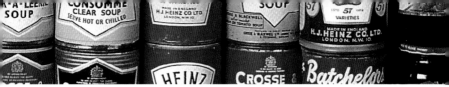

Glossary

We have tried to be as straightforward as possible, but there are always a few technical terms that you can't manage without, so here goes...

ALTERNATIVE DESIGN
A reaction to the throwaway 1960s, linked with the stirrings of the green movement in the 70s. Concerned with minimal, noncommercial, appropriate design for those in need.

ANTI-DESIGN
A rejection of the certainties of modernism that took root in the 1960s, particularly in Italy, following from the fun element of Pop design. Matured into the Memphis group in the 1980s. Often intended to surprise or shock.

ART DECO
Primarily a geometric design style that was a reaction to the florid, organic style of Art Nouveau, which declined as modernity took over in the early twentieth century. Its origins were in the 1925 Exposition Internationale des Arts Décoratifs, Industriels et Modernes, held in Paris.

ART NOUVEAU
The first design style that did not look back to an earlier one. It was typified by swirling plant-inspired shapes that could be applied to a wide range of products, architecture, and graphics, and enjoyed a brief but widespread popularity.

BAROQUE
An ornate, florid style intended to overwhelm the viewer with visual effect. It evolved into Rococo in the early eighteenth century.

BIOMORPHIC DESIGN
See Organic Design.

CAD
Computer-Aided Design.

CLASSICISM, NEOCLASSICAL
Revivals of Greek and Roman principles of design, usually architectural.

CONSTRUCTIVISM
Constructivism emerged as a distinctive new machine-age, anti-art principle in Russia in the period that followed World War I and the 1917 Revolution. It allowed for radical new ideas in art and design. Its artifacts were produced by the assembly of forms or materials, often geometric and simple. It spanned sculpture, graphics, fashion, and architecture.

CORPORATE IDENTITY
The adoption by large companies, often transnational, of an organized identity that is applied to all the visual aspects of the company's promotional material, advertising, packaging, and so on.

DADA
A nonsense name, which was adopted to describe the aims of an artistic and literary movement triggered by the disillusionment and disgust engendered by World War I. Although mainly an art phenomenon, its original ideas were to have an influence on graphic design in due course.

DESIGN
A tricky one. Read this book, starting with the introduction.

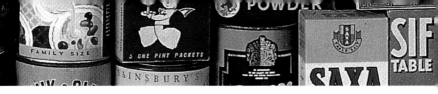

ERGONOMICS
The designing of things to fit human need and operation, rather than imposing uncomfortable positions.

FUNCTIONALISM
A tenet of modernism was that "Form followed Function," i.e., there was no place for unnecessary ornament or decoration.

FUTURISM
An Italian-inspired revolutionary movement that was briefly influential around 1910–14. Its adherents insisted that all the creative arts could be harnessed to make a new world by embracing new ideas and technology.

GRAPHIC DESIGN
A 1950s term that originally referred to the design of printed matter, but now also includes electronic forms of communication that use type and images.

HIGH-TECH
A design style that became popular with furniture designers, interior designers, and architects in the 1980s, embracing industrial materials and favoring an undecorated "rivets and all" look.

MACHINE AGE
Refers to the mechanistic qualities of design derived from machine forms, i.e., functional, efficient. The opposite of the Arts and Crafts esthetic.

MINIMALISM
The reduction of the elements of design (color, form, texture, and decoration) to a minimum.

MODERN MOVEMENT
A vague term that describes the twentieth-century preference for new forms, often geometric and undecorated, and applied mainly to graphic design, architecture, and furniture. Associated with rational, unemotional thinking.

ORGANIC DESIGN
Design derived from forms occurring in nature, usually involving soft, curved shapes.

POP ART, POP DESIGN
The visual equivalent of 60s pop music, associated with the youth culture that celebrated the everyday and ignored the established principles of "good" taste, art, and design.

POSTMODERN
A catch-all word to describe the shift of many aspects of the arts in the mid- to late 1970s, that allowed its followers openly to use derivative sources for their inspiration, but in a more complex way than a straight revival. It reflects the plurality, and multitaste, multioption lifestyle of much contemporary (Western) culture.

RETRO
The deliberate revival of a past style, but usually one that is still in recent memory rather than an antique one.

STREAMLINING
Originally the functional application of aerodynamic shapes to moving vehicles in the 1930s, but a style that became applied to many non-moving consumer goods for purely styling purposes.

TYPOGRAPHY
The way type (lettering) is arranged on a page, or more recently on the computer monitor or TV screen. The principles of typography have their roots in traditional printing methods.

VERNACULAR DESIGN
The borrowing of a traditional style, often architectural, adapting its use or applying its decorative qualities to another design.

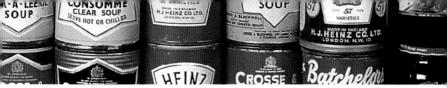

Index

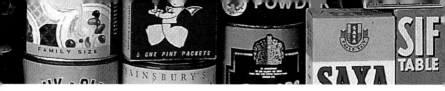

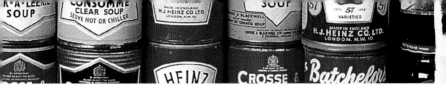